HERODOTUS
AN INTERPRETATIVE ESSAY

HERODOTUS

AN INTERPRETATIVE ESSAY

———

CHARLES W. FORNARA

CLARENDON PRESS · OXFORD

1971

Oxford University Press, Ely House, London W.1

GLASGOW   NEW YORK   TORONTO   MELBOURNE   WELLINGTON
CAPE TOWN   SALISBURY   IBADAN   NAIROBI   DAR ES SALAAM   LUSAKA   ADDIS ABABA
BOMBAY   CALCUTTA   MADRAS   KARACHI   LAHORE   DACCA
KUALA LUMPUR   SINGAPORE   HONG KONG   TOKYO

PRINTED IN GREAT BRITAIN
BY WILLIAM CLOWES AND SONS, LIMITED
LONDON, BECCLES AND COLCHESTER

To my wife
Nancy Pattison Fornara

For as I am, in reality, the founder of a new province of writing, so I am at liberty to make what laws I please therein. And these laws, my readers, whom I consider as my subjects, are bound to believe in and to obey; with which that they may readily and cheerfully comply, I do hereby assure them that I shall principally regard their ease and advantage in all such institutions; for I do not, like a *jure divino* tyrant, imagine that they are my slaves or my commodity. I am, indeed, set over them for their own good only, and was created for their use, and not they for mine. Nor do I doubt, while I make their interest the great rule of my writings, they will unanimously concur in supporting my dignity, and in rendering me all the honour I shall deserve or desire.

FIELDING, *Tom Jones*, Book II, Chapter I.

PREFACE

ECAUSE Herodotus' work is the first of its kind, the
question of how he came to write it is of more than pass-
ing interest and importance. And although it is un-
fashionable nowadays to attempt to extract from Herodotus'
Histories the record of his development, the attempt is worth
making because it focuses attention on an aspect of his genius
which it is easy to take for granted and which, when taken for
granted, leads easily to misinterpretation of his intentions. To
historians, Herodotus is the Father of History about whose
lapses we can afford to be charitable because his followers
perfected the genre. To literary critics, his book is a 'work of
art' the genesis of which is relatively unimportant.* Both
schools of thought seem to me to misjudge Herodotus'
achievement because of general presuppositions and prejudices actually irrelevant.

I should add that although I have read the literature on
the subject as conscientiously as possible, the persuasion that
brevity is a virtue and that the argument in the text must provide its justification without help or hindrance from debates
in footnotes has led me to keep bibliographical citation and
polemic about all but major points to a minimum.

Rehoboth, Massachusetts   C.W.F.

* H. R. Immerwahr, *Form and Thought in Herodotus* (Cleveland, 1966), p. 8.

CONTENTS

ABBREVIATIONS

I

UNITARIANS, SEPARATISTS, AND BOOK II

ERODOTUS' work is a universal history on a massive scale. That it possesses a history of its own reaching back through a considerable number of years can hardly be denied. The *Histories* contain an enormous amount of information; the greater part of it must have been gathered in laborious and time-consuming ways. The series of travels undertaken by Herodotus around the periphery of the civilized world as well as throughout Greece and, finally, to southern Italy mark stages of his life as well as sections of his work. And whether we suppose that he embarked on these voyages of discovery intending to write the very book he has bequeathed us, as some believe, or whether we do not, supposing instead that he set himself originally a less ambitious goal, some literary activity directly related to the work we now possess must have been an immediate consequence of those travels. For we are not to imagine that Herodotus failed at once, during the time he made his inquiries or very shortly thereafter, to cast into prose the burden of his discoveries about each of the places he visited. That being so, the important conclusion follows that Herodotus either wrote what we have piece by piece over the years or instead wrote something similar, at least in substance, out of which he later fashioned the final work. In either case, it would be probable *a priori* that the *Histories* preserve signs of intellectual development; that they reflect shifts of interest and different approaches to the problems of authorship which will have been the natural concomitants of Herodotus' expanding vision during his years of inquiry and writing.

On similarly general grounds, it is also reasonable to expect that the work Herodotus left us is a different thing from what at the start of his career he might have predicted. Were not his plans and preconceptions altered subtly and drastically by his reactions to the very travels and investigations with which he occupied himself over the course of his life? Whatever his initial intent may have been, the unpredictable course of his progressive enlightenment must, one would think, have affected it and have helped to shape it. When, for example, did Herodotus conceive of a train of cause and effect so far-reaching that an act of injustice by Croesus could be considered as having set in motion the events which culminated in the Persian War? Was it before or after his trip to Sardes or to Delphi? Again, Herodotus did not live in a vacuum. Though it may be impossible to gauge the effect upon him of the literary achievements of his contemporaries in that remarkably productive generation, some literary contact and stimulation there surely was. Some effect on Herodotus there must have been; we should allow for the possibility that his responses resulted in substantive changes in his intentions and plans. Finally, he did not inherit but created the form of art his *Histories* represent. The gulf that separates Herodotus' achievement from the productions of his predecessors and contemporaries, so far as they can be judged,[1] is plausibly explained, if not necessarily explained, by a kind of dialectic between his progressively ambitious intent and the increasing complexity of the problems he was thereby obligated to deal with. The most original achievements of great artists entail some prior development. *Dubliners* preceded *Ulysses*, *The Flying Dutchman* preceded *Tristan and Isolde*; Gibbon's great work expanded as if endowed with a life of its own.[2] For Herodotus, though the *Histories* is 'one

---

[1] See Dionysius of Halicarnassus, *de Thuc.* 5. Cf. F. Jacoby, *Abhandlungen zur griechischen Geschichtschreibung* (Leiden, 1956), p. 180, n. 10, T. S. Brown, *American Historical Review* 54 (1954), 837.

[2] Gibbon, *Memoirs of My Life*, ed. G. A. Bonnard (London, 1966), pp. 164, 181.

work', it is also the work of his life. A combination of reasons therefore suggests that Herodotus' *Histories* contain within themselves, clearly or faintly, some signs of his intellectual development.

General considerations of this kind seem corroborated by some singular and oft-recognized features of Herodotus' work. His every reader has noted the ethnographical 'digressions', has sensed the relative independence of his account of Egypt in Book II, has felt the degree of difference in his treatment of the Great War of Xerxes in VII–IX from what precedes it—even if it is difficult to define the nature of this shift in more than quantitative terms. That all of this is integrated, like the heads of the hydra in the body of that mythical beast, does not diminish the ostensible probability that Herodotus ran through a succession of interests which had been central to him at different stages of his career. Though, for example, it is possible to justify the inclusion of Book II, his account of Egypt, into the totality of his *Histories*, that justification leaves unaffected the clear impression that Herodotus wrote that book guided by ethnographical interests. The likelihood is that, to the extent that he considered the matter at all, he viewed himself while he was writing it as that kind of author. Thus the question arises whether Herodotus at that time was already stimulated to become the historian of the Persian Wars. A historian of the Persian Wars might perhaps have been induced to write something about Egypt if he interpreted his subject with the broadest possible latitude. But it is hard to believe that his possession of such a goal would not have precluded him from writing an account of Egypt which in conception and scale amounts to a book in its own right and essentially has nothing to do either with its absorption by the Greek foe, Persia, or with the war between the Persians and the Greeks. There is a natural correlation between one's goal and the way it is attacked. Conversely, it may be more than accidental that this massive contribution to ethnography is closely comparable in treatment and subject with the genre of literature attempted by the predecessors and contemporaries of Herodotus.

It is not merely fanciful, therefore, to suppose that Herodotus' work may contain within it some of the traces of his own development as writer and artist. Indeed, that conclusion is implicit in the fact that students of Herodotus are unable to define his work as having been the result of his investigations of a single theme.[3] They have differed on what precisely the subject may have been, one scholar even suggesting that the work is too diffuse to have a proper subject.[4] It was, pre-eminently, Felix Jacoby, in an epoch-making study of Herodotus published in 1913,[5] who attempted to explain this confusing situation by postulating a developmental hypothesis. According to Jacoby, Herodotus passed through a series of stages reflected in the different subjects of the *Histories* which, initially, were independent. Beginning as a geographer and ethnographer, Herodotus, on this view, then became the author of a Persian history, the *Persikoi logoi*, and finally evolved into the historian of the Persian Wars.[6] This hypothesis, taking its starting-point from the identification of the categorically different 'subjects' of the author, explained them as the record of his development from the follower of Hecataeus into the original historian whose *Histories* is the synthesis of the work of his career.

In recent years, however, the 'genetic' or analytic approach to works of art has given ground to the 'unitarian' approach, a style of literary criticism rendered especially popular in reaction to the excesses of the other as manifested, especially, in Homeric scholarship. And so Herodotus' work has been viewed as a 'unity' in which his 'excursuses' into ethnography as represented by the apparently disparate *logoi* find their explanation not in Herodotus' chronological development but in their integral importance to the work as a

---

[3] See *Lustrum* 11 (1966), 86f. for recent bibliography.

[4] F. Focke, *Herodot als Historiker, Tübinger Beiträge zur Altertumswissenschaft, Heft* 1 (Stuttgart, 1927), pp. 8, 13f., 48f.

[5] *RE Suppl.* II.

[6] Ibid., 341ff., especially 353ff.

whole.[7] Instead, therefore, of explaining the whole in terms of the parts, the parts find their explanation in terms of the whole. It is unfortunate that these two approaches have been viewed as alternative explanations of how Herodotus' *Histories* came about. They are not incompatible with each other since really they serve different ends. To the extent that the 'unitarian' approach to Herodotus has become the substitute rather than the complement of the genetic has there been a serious methodological step backwards in the study of Herodotus since the time of the appearance of Jacoby's work.

If it was beneficial to be reminded that Herodotus' history is not an aggregation of *disiecta membra*, it was not because the contrary was claimed, at least in our century, but because our habituation to viewing the *Histories* in the light of the likely genesis of their parts, as originally separate and independent *logoi*, tended to obscure our appreciation of their masterly subordination. Unfortunately, the reaction went too far. The idea has been deprecated that Herodotus' intellectual development might explain problematical features in his work, apparently because assumptions of this kind are felt to diminish the aesthetical integrity of his accomplishment.[8] Max Pohlenz, for example, was not content to demonstrate that the history carries so many signs of the subordination of the parts to the whole that the work as we have it was planned for the form in which we have it and is therefore the product of a 'unified' conception. He was also unwilling to allow that this unified work consisted of parts of initially independent origin. The work, he maintained, was not only unified in the disposition of its parts. These parts were themselves originated by Herodotus with a view to their ultimate incorporation in the whole.[9] Herodotus did not begin as a geographer, did not go through an ethnographical

[7] See especially M. Pohlenz, *Herodot, der erste Geschichtschreiber des Abendlandes*, Neue Wege zur Antike, II. Reihe, Heft 7/8 (Leipzig, 1937), *passim*.

[8] See, for example, F. Egermann, *Neue Jahrbücher für Antike und deutsche Bildung* 1 (1938), 191, for a comparatively clear statement of this attitude; see also the Preface.

[9] Pohlenz, op. cit., p. 70.

stage, did not plan to write a history of Persia. He was our historian *ab initio*.[10]

That Herodotus began his career with the preconceived design of completing it with the work we now have is a theoretical possibility—though there are sufficient reasons to which allusion has already been made to suggest that it is psychologically improbable. What it is important to realize, however, is that such a conclusion as this is a consequence not of the unitarian argument but of an aesthetical prejudice. The 'unity' of a work need imply nothing as to its genesis. Indeed, that argument from 'unity' is altogether misleading. Terms such as 'unity', 'inner unity', etc., are too fluid to be applied to such complex questions as the composition of a literary work. Although we may speak of the unity of a painting, a poem, a musical composition, or a history, the term lacks scientific rigour, to say the least. Works have unity in a relative, not an absolute degree. It would be absurd to maintain that Herodotus' work, or any other book, is an absolute unity or even 'a unity'—in the sense that it consists of components inevitably interlocked from which one could not be subtracted or others added without impairment of the whole. (It would be more useful to apply the term comparatively, to observe that Herodotus' work, when compared to those of others, Thucydides, Sallust, Tacitus, Ammianus, seems far less unified according to the way we normally use the term.) One simply means by words of this kind that a given work is coherent, another way of saying that it contains nothing obviously or inescapably irreconcilable with it. Unity, in short, is a term as misleading as it is overworked. Though it appears to suggest the presence of a positive quality in what it is predicated of, it nevertheless merely constates the absence of some such negative quality as, for instance, chaos. The 'unity' of Herodotus' *Histories* (and the plural seems apt) cannot therefore be invoked, as it has been, as a principle which solves the problems of the composition of this work. We cannot say, because it is a unity, that what it contains must have been originated in order to subserve it. Although we may, with a little good will, *justify* the presence of Book II on Egypt in the *Histories* by assuming it to be a consequence of Herodotus' desire to inform the reader of this new accession to the Persian Empire,[11] and although we may even say, hypothetically, that Book II is in substance as well as formally a component of the *Histories* not disunited from the rest, it is specious reasoning to designate thereby the whole a 'unity' and proceed to assert that Book II owed its genesis to the part it plays in the Grand Design. For in this light it is difficult to conceive of anything Herodotus might have written about the history of the civilized world prior to writing the work we now have which, if he had then inserted it, would not be susceptible to explanation in this manner, especially if his theme is interpreted with the broadest possible latitude and Herodotus' sense of relevancy is imagined to be the captive of his 'wide-eyed enthusiasm'.

The fact that Herodotus' *Histories* are not composed of *disiecta membra* arbitrarily stitched together without mutual accommodation no more makes the work a unity in a sense that permits conclusions about its composition than the presence in it of such quasi-independent narratives as that on Egypt makes it disunited or capricious. Herodotus wrote this work under the impression that it was capable of being read between two covers without causing aesthetical indigestion; he took pains, and showed genius, in subordinating the parts to the whole. It may be more reasonable to account for them by postulating some order of development in Herodotus' intellect and aims than by appealing to a higher unity that subordinates them. Particularly is this so in view of the rather unique kind of unity Herodotus' *Histories* display.

In most cases, the unity of a work consists in the treatment of a unitary subject, an object of study, essentially nuclear, capable of succinct formulation. The intent of an author

---

[11] Ibid., p. 70. The claim there is made that Herodotus wrote Book II in the same spirit that led Mommsen in his *Roman History* to include a chapter on Carthage before describing the Punic War. The analogy is imperfect.

prior to writing a work (however much the work may be elaborated in the process of being written) is, so far as the subject of that work is concerned, self-evident. It would have been safe to say, for example, and unnecessary to argue, even if he did not tell us, that Thucydides' history of the Peloponnesian War presupposes an originally conceived intent on his part to chronicle that war which preceded and guided his collection of material. Even the material chronologically outside the framework of the war, his discussion of the *archaeologia*, of the Pentecontaetia, of early Sicilian history, follows naturally enough from his conception of what the reader needs to know in order to understand the war. Even when we cannot explain his inclusion of material on the grounds that it is strictly relevant to his subject, as with his treatment of Pausanias and Themistocles, we are under no compulsion to assume that it is anything more than a digression as the term normally is used. If we turn to Herodotus, however, it is clear that the 'unity' of his work is of a different order. It is manifestly not the elaboration of a unitary subject. When, as here, the description of the work becomes the description of its parts since no one of the parts subsumes all the others, then the work is not a 'unity' in the usually accepted sense. The normal conclusion, that the work corresponds to an initial desire to write it anterior to and explanatory of the parts, no longer follows. It is with Herodotus rather a matter of his *unification* of different subjects, as even the unitarians have concluded. Otto Regenbogen, for example, speaks of three principles of composition, *Aufbaumitteln*, which in his view compel the whole into a unity. They are, first, 'the thought of the struggle between East and West, the national opposition between Greeks and barbarians; secondly, most comprehensive for the structure as a whole, the thought of the extent and growth of the Persian Empire, . . . and, finally, *von innen her durchleuchtend, an krisenhaften Stellen deutlich hervortretend*, the ethicometaphysical, the religious motive.'[12] The logic behind the

[12] *Die Antike* 6 (1930), 245.

assertion that these compel the whole into unity is not self-evident. They seem rather to provide a listing in as inclusive a phraseology as possible of two of Herodotus' subjects—the *Persikoi logoi* and the Great War—and an allusion to his religiosity. Is the work a unity because of the presence in it of these topics or because he has managed to bind them up together deftly? How can they be the *means* of unity? The mental leap from 'This is a work consisting of x, y, and z' to 'This work is a unity because of the presence of x, y, and z' seems arbitrary. One could also state, perhaps more justly, that 'This work is not a unity because of the presence of x and y' or that 'In spite of x and y Herodotus has written a work which is unified.' In any case, the important conclusion is that the kind of work Herodotus wrote does not in virtue of its 'unity' suggest, as does Thucydides', that it has evolved in the natural elaboration of a single subject which thereby predetermined the unity of the work. Indeed, a contrary in-ference seems required. Herodotus' 'co-ordinate' subjects are incapable of being subsumed by the kind of elementary and specific concept which could plausibly have inspired him to begin this work and out of subservience to which the genesis of these subjects could be explained.

As a critical approach to the finished work the unitarian view yields valuable results in permitting us to form a clear idea of the means Herodotus has taken to synthesize and unify his material or, to view it another way, of the intel-lectual and moral concerns which are the dominating and unifying motives of his work. But as a hypothesis of the origin of the parts of that work it is ultimately question-begging. It succeeds not in explaining but in justifying, where it does not merely describe, the very peculiarities in Herodotus' work—the ethnographical sections, the Persian history, the mono-graph of VII–IX—which most require explanation and which it was at least the function of Jacoby's hypothesis to explain. Beyond this, however, an even more notable failure of this hypothesis, which 'explains' the parts by reference to the 'unity' containing them, is its deficiency in being able to provide, what at all costs it must, a plausible explanation for the genesis of the whole.

With the substitution of a unitarian view of Herodotus' creation for a developmental hypothesis, Herodotus' history becomes that curious thing, the outcome of a plan formulated prior to the research and travels of which the work is the outcome! The unitarians are actually arguing not that Herodotus commenced with a plan which resulted in his having written the *Histories*—for this, in essence, is also the genetic view, always remembering that the 'plan' evolved continuously in the course of his career—but that the *Histories* themselves, in conception if not execution, were the 'plan' by which he was inspired. For this is implied in the assumption that Herodotus was prompted to engage in his travels and research in order to write the book we now possess. He went to Egypt, in other words, intending to write Book II more or less as it stands—not a work on ethnography or whatever we may choose to call it. The assumption tacitly made by the unitarians is that Herodotus had the framework of this colossal structure already in his head before he underwent the experiences creative of his greatest intellectual growth and before he collected the facts so essential to his theme. It is much to infer simply from the fact that the *Histories* are well organized. It is an assumption blandly retrojecting to a period in Herodotus' youth the wisdom, ambition, and revolutionary vision which more properly would be expected of him in the riper years of his creativity. It is a truism that plans even well made are incalculably affected by unforeseen problems and possibilities raised in that span of time an author devotes to the composition of his work. In Herodotus' case that span consisted of decades, and in them he acquired new knowledge and experience.

Even the motivation ascribed to Herodotus for having written the *Histories* by those who reject a developmental hypothesis seems curiously unrealistic. Herodotus is assumed to have responded not to the currents of his own time, when actually he wrote his work, but to emotions and considerations prevalent some forty years before he wrote it. This is, of course, a consequence of the necessity of having him take his plan with him on his travels. Hence the assertion of Wolfgang Schadewaldt that Herodotus was inspired to write about the Persian Wars, the opposition between Greek and barbarian, not in Athens of the forties or thirties but, much earlier, in Halicarnassus. For 'that opposition more markedly dominated the atmosphere of Asia Minor in Herodotos' youth.'[13] The truth of this assertion—that such was the feeling in Halicarnassus shortly after the event—is doubtful.[14] More important, the idea that what Herodotus was supposedly excited by at an early age could have become the driving motivation behind the work of his mature years provides an example of anachronistic thinking. A general consideration of this kind, based not at all on Herodotus, is incapable of explaining or motivating the specific work under consideration. If it is reasonable to suppose that Herodotus at the age of four or five was moved by the general furore in Halicarnassus in the year(s) after Artemisia's return because of tales about Artemisia's bravery, the Persian defeat, or even the Greek victory, that is no more than what other little boys also felt. If he had been old enough to begin writing the *Histories* contemporaneously with that event, it would be a different matter. Such explanations as these, in fact, are not explanations at all. They are mere preconditions which explain equally, or leave equally unexplained, Herodotus, Charon of Lampsacus, and Dionysius of Miletus. But these were authors of very different kinds of works, and it is the particular work which requires explanation. It is not to be achieved by shifting the problem back to Herodotus' boyhood.

The test of any hypothesis is that it provides a credible

[13] *Die Antike* 10 (1934), 157.
[14] It is an unsupported inference from Herodotus himself. The grand conception of ancestral rivalry between East and West is not implicit in a two-year war between Persia and the Greeks of the Balkans. It may be suggested that our own certitude of the prior existence of this theme may derive from our prior digestion of Herodotus and, more important, because the many centuries that have since elapsed give substance to the antithesis.

explanation of the phenomena involved in the object of study. Retrojection of the problem does not provide a cogent explanation of why actually he wrote what he did. Though it may seem reasonable to conclude from his work that he intended to write it as he has, it is surely a different matter to suppose that he reached this decision *in vacuo*, before, in other words, he collected and gave shape to the preponderance of the material which it contains. The assumption is gratuitous, seems implausible, and explains nothing. Would an author who at the start of his career intended to write about the Persian War have defined the task to himself so broadly as to thread the labyrinthine course of research and travel his book represents? Anyone, perhaps, could have selected such a subject as the war of 480 B.C. (though it awaited Herodotus, more than forty years after the event, to undertake it). But only one broadly versed in the history of virtually the entire world could have undertaken to deal with that subject, or have considered the possibility of treating it, on the stupendous scale of Herodotus. The causes of the Persian War do not lead back to an unjust act by Croesus, as simple reflection should serve to convince— except to one who is both the master of Lydian history and desirous of including it. The history of Egypt is of a different order of relevance to such a subject, if, indeed, it is relevant at all, than are the ships that were the 'beginning of evil' (V. 97) sent by the Athenians to Ionia under the command of Melanthius in 499 B.C. Herodotus' travels explain the inclusion of information of this kind. But his travels cannot be explained as subservient to his desire to write about the Persian War unless we suppose that he defined his task with such latitude that in fact he had no plan at all.

That a description of the work before us, therefore, could become also an explanation of its genesis is a testimony more to the heat with which unitarians responded to the prior neglect of this most important aspect of Herodotus' achievement than to any intrinsic justification of such method. The unitarian view provides a proper estimate of Herodotus' skill at the final stage of his career. It is the necessary complement of a developmental hypothesis such as that of Jacoby and his followers whose purpose is to diagnose the problematical features in Herodotus' work. The one describes what we possess; the other attempts to explain how what we do possess could have come into the world.

However idiosyncratic and novel in its totality, Herodotus' work contains elements exhibiting characteristics which are paralleled in the works of his predecessors and contemporaries. These elements are more primitive in conception and in execution than the rich and complex portions of Herodotus' history in which they are embedded. They are not an inevitable feature of the work as even the unitarians define its burden. They testify to Herodotus' evolution from such a writer as his older and even younger colleagues, who wrote from within a tradition of small and numerous books[15] devoted to geography, like Hecataeus', and ethnography, like Hellanicus',[16] or, more properly, devoted to a subject including both in various mixtures. That Herodotus began as they did and came gradually to contemplate ever more ambitious undertakings culminating in the work that binds them all or nearly all together in a 'unified' work of art is at least a supposition that roots Herodotus into the literary tradition of his time and explains the presence in his work of material evidently gathered for its own sake.[17]

Unfortunately, both the proponents and the critics of the idea of a developmental hypothesis have obscured its merits, or at least some of them, by applying it, in support and in attack, with a rigidity that is excessive and unnatural. Little allowance is made for the fluidity of what in our proclivity to abstraction we call the 'genre' of prose literature in Herodotus' time. For example, the idea that Herodotus at an early point in his career might have been a 'follower' of Hecataeus is equivalent in the minds of some to the belief

---

[15] See Jacoby, *Abhandlungen*, p. 186.   [16] Ibid., pp. 191, 198.
[17] The question of *scale* deserves attention. Are modern examples of encyclopedic works a proper parallel to what is predicated of Herodotus?

that, on this view, he must have intended to follow Hecataeus precisely. Thus there has been a marked and unrealistic insistence that for a hypothesis of this type to be workable, Herodotus must arguably have undergone a metamorphosis from one neatly precise stage to another—as, for example, from 'geographer' to 'historian'. Jacoby, for instance, may well have overrated the initial formal dependence of Herodotus on Hecataeus. His critics have rightly shown that the evidence does not support the notion that he began as a geographer intending to write a *periodos ges*. At the same time the conclusion that because Herodotus was evidently not a 'pure' geographer he was therefore a 'historian' and so must have been 'our historian' *ab initio* is illusory.[18] Arguments about such terms as 'geographer' and 'historian' and questions about when properly one is this or that are more in place in theoretical discussions than in historiography. To wonder when Herodotus became a 'historian' after having been a 'geographer' or 'ethnographer' is to insist upon a rigour of terminology out of place except as a professional label in a modern university. A hypothesis of Herodotus' development needs to be more concerned than it has been with his interests and his intent than with his 'nature'. It needs, as well, to take into account the fact that such mun-

---

[18] The objection to Jacoby's view seems to be merely semantical. Thus he is confuted because Herodotus never was a '*reiner Geograph*' (Regenbogen, *Die Antike* 6 (1930), 216, quoted with approval by R. Walzer, *Gnomon* 6 (1930), 578, n. 2). Pohlenz, *op. cit.*, p. 73, poses this question: 'Was Herodotus initially led by historical interests or did he begin as a geographer or, indeed, as a collector of curiosities?' Elsewhere he asks the question, with its submerged negative, whether Herodotus ever had 'pure geographical interests' (p. 78). The word 'pure' comes up again and again. But Jacoby did not suggest that Herodotus was a 'pure geographer'.—A similarly treacherous step is involved in the assertion of W. Schmid-O. Stählin, *Griechische Literaturgeschichte* I. 2. 584, following Focke, op cit., pp. 38ff., that because Herodotus was not merely an 'ethnographer' but also a 'historian' when he went on his travels—for he collected a mass of 'historical' material in Egypt—it follows that he already contemplated a history of Persia. To this chaos of definitions was added another when Kurt von Fritz, *Die Griechische Geschichtschreibung* (Berlin, 1967) I. 158ff., concluded that Herodotus was not really a historian when he wrote Book II. See below.

dane considerations as the expectations of his readers are also determinants of what he wrote.

The point may be illustrated by a brief examination of the discussion about Book II by Kurt von Fritz in his recent massive study of Herodotus.[19] He attempts to show that Herodotus, in this early stage of his career represented by Book II, was 'above all' a geographer interested in the problem of the sources of the Nile[20] and not yet a 'historian'.[21] The total effect of Book II upon me does not suggest that the priority of interests are as von Fritz represents them. More important, however, is the fact, evident in von Fritz's discussion as in others, that Herodotus' work is treated as if it were the product of an author completely dissociated from his milieu. The massive attention devoted to Herodotus' literary antecedents is only matched by disregard for the other important term in the equation—the people for whom this work was written. For no allowance is made for the fact that Herodotus wrote his book expecting it to be read by his contemporaries. Inevitably he had a definite public in mind. To a certain degree, at least, their expectations must have weighed with him as did also (though it is perhaps the same thing) the requirements of the 'genre' in which he was writing. Herodotus, however he may have pleased himself, intended primarily to publish his work, or give lectures from it, for the pleasure and edification of others. What would they minimally have expected from such a work? To extrapolate from Book II or from a prominent passage in it the priority of Herodotus' interests without regard to his having been a flesh and blood traveller, not yet a 'classic', and so necessarily attuned to contemporary expectations and obliged to deal with already ventilated questions, is to lose perspective. Could one bring home to Greece a narrative about Egypt without comment on the most striking and famous feature of the natural landscape of that exotic land or without consideration of already newsworthy and controversial problems

<hr>

[19] Ibid.   [20] Ibid., 139.   [21] Ibid., 177f.

connected with it? Geographical questions about the regu-
larity and size of the continents or the sources of the Nile
were obvious and inevitable. We can hardly doubt that
Herodotus' reading of Hecataeus and others provided him
with ready-made, indeed, indispensable topics. That he went
with a critical mind to Egypt, intending if possible to improve
on his predecessors seems self-evident. His audience, moreover,
as he well knew, would have expected it from him. Geography
seems to have been the staple of the menu. Not until Herodotus, apparently, did it cease to be the main course. In this
context, therefore, what is especially noteworthy about Book
II is that the abstract questions of geography have receded in
interest, yielding their erstwhile central position to ethnographical and historical matters. For we must look at Book II
—which unquestionably is a 'unity' in the sense we normally
use the word—as a whole, and characterize Herodotus'
interests by weighing the balanced account of Egypt he has
written. What he *is* is certainly clear. He is the author of a
lively book about Egypt, its geography, the people, their
customs, religion, and history.

To ask, therefore, 'What is Herodotus at this stage?' is
to find a classification and lose the author. Merely asking
whether he is a 'geographer' or 'historian' prejudices our
judgement of what he is. It distorts the question at issue
by focusing attention on such arid matters as whether a
'pure' geographer could have written this passage or a 'true'
historian have written that. Von Fritz, for example, concludes that Herodotus was not a 'historian' because his
account of the early dynasts stems not from priests 'highly
placed and highly educated'[22] but rather from less eminent
people and because, in addition, Herodotus did not pursue
Forschungen in history as he did in geography.[23] According
to von Fritz, 'historical criticism is the single quality that
makes a historian a historian."[24] Whatever the merits of
this definition, it should be clear that Herodotus' 'critical
method' as applied to Hecataeus was an inevitable aspect of

[22] Ibid., 178.   [23] Ibid., 177.   [24] Ibid., 178.

his treatment of the conclusions of his predecessor. He attempted to dispute them. On the other hand, his attempt to sketch what in spite of his miserable sources remains the history of the more important kings of Egypt is 'uncritical' only because it involved no polemic of this kind. Against whom? The issue is not the quality of Herodotus' sources or his difficulty in providing us with a more veracious historical record. It is that he considered it a part of his task to provide an historical dimension in his account. And here, so far as we can tell, he is his own man rather more than the product of a tradition. Whether that makes him a geographer, an ethnographer, or a historian or, as seems more reasonable if less precise, an author combining a variety of such interests, what is crucial is that he is an author of a kind different from what he will become at the end of his career as represented by the final work as a whole. Indeed, the chief interest of Book II (for our purposes) is that it not only shows us what he was at an early stage but also what he was not yet become. The natural supposition that Book II essentially as it stands is the result of a venture to Egypt independent of and prior to the later plan eventuating into his history is confirmed by more than its 'excursus-like' nature within the history as a whole. Differences in technique and conception mark it off from other books that, whatever their origin, are so dominated by Herodotus' final plan and preoccupations that they must have been written, or rewritten, in the final draft. Book I would probably be considered by most students to be an uncontroversial example of such a book. Let us, then, view them side by side.

It is apparent at once on the technical level, in Herodotus' organization of the material contained in it, that Book I is more complex than II not only in the disposition of what is related but also in its variegated texture. Book II is straightforward and uncomplicated in its description, section by section, of the geography, customs, and history of Egypt. Book I effortlessly unites a mass of information culled over a wide period of time and from a diversity of source. The

affairs of Lydia and Persia or, rather, of Croesus and Cyrus—
a biographical orientation notably different from anything in
II—are the subjects of this book; and they are dexterously
intertwined with episodes of Athenian and Spartan history,
with information derived from Delphi and even Taenarum.
The loosely associative technique of organization permitting
relevant digressions differs markedly from the purely linear
order manifested in II. Unlike II, again, Book I looks beyond
itself, as it were, in the connections specifically made
(whether forcedly or not) with the antecedents of the Persian
Wars: it is written with an eye to the fortunes of the Greek
cities on the coastland befriended or conquered by Croesus
and then by Cyrus as well as to the dominant states in
Greece which eventually will be the strength of the western
defence. The relations of Egyptian and Greek were un-
clouded by this sort of antagonism. But even that perspective
is lacking. Such a consideration as the ultimate conflict is
irrelevant to his account of Egypt. Most striking of all, and
hardly to be explained by the subject matter, is the *utter
absence* in II of the moral or philosophical element, Regenbogen's religious motive, exemplified in I by the Solon-
Croesus story, though not by that alone. Herodotus is in
Book I intent upon expounding his philosophy of history; it
informs and dominates his account of the fall of Croesus and
the rise and fall of Cyrus. Book II is free of it. Eloquent as was
the history of Egypt of the transience of human fortune, it is
no more than merely implicit in his account.[25] Furthermore,
difficult as it is to be precise about something so indefinite as
the *persona* exhibited by Herodotus in I, it is none the less
different from that displayed in II. In I he is unobtrusive and

---

[25] The important distinction made by Jacoby, *Abhandlungen*, p. 194, between
Charon of Lampsacus and Herodotus is also valid as a distinction between
Book II and the rest of the work. 'Charon relates the facts known to him in their
normal sequence, each for itself; and even when he finds a higher meaning in
them, he keeps to the specific instance; Herodotus conceived of the opposition of
Greek and Persian as an inner unity, constructed it by degrees, and selected and
arranged his material to achieve it with great effect.' We see in Book II, in other
words, the general level of narrative art before Herodotus lifted it to a higher
plane.

gravely serious; his dramatically rich portrayal is undisturbed by protestations about his dependence on his sources
or his indifference to their truth. He is completely the master
of his material, choosing among conflicting versions and relegating some to silence.[26] Perhaps that is why the 'entertainment' Herodotus provides in I is of a different order from
what he displays in II. It is dramatic and serious. Even the
adventure of Arion (I. 23f.) is presented more for the magnificent picture of his plight than for the miracle of his rescue.
Herodotus is a dramatic author, not a teller of tales.

In Book II Herodotus has not only another and more primitive technique but, above all, another *persona* as well. He
is the Traveller. He is telling us what he has seen. Clever,
paradoxical, combative,[27] his book is a showpiece of his skill.
But his skill is devoted to superficial ends, not the least
element in them being self-display.[28] He wishes his audience
to know that he is wiser than the Ionians in geographical
matters (II. 15, 20), and he is contemptuous of them in a
prideful and polemical spirit nowhere present in I. In
ethnographical matters he is keen to point out astonishing
variations in customs with a taste for paradox not unmixed
with humour. Women in Egypt urinate as they do the world
over but Herodotus wanted to turn a clever phrase (II. 35. 3).
In telling his audience that the Greeks were children in comparison with the Egyptians (II. 51ff.), he is not merely adumbrating a theory but pursuing destructive criticism of the
general and unconsidered assumptions of his parochial contemporaries with much the same feeling, probably, of any
sophist making a shambles of self-evident truths. That he is
being seriously anti-Greek or pro-Egyptian is an unjustified
and naïve assumption. Herodotus was on show, and the
topics he selected had appeal. Even Homer is brought in
(II. 112ff.)—with a paradoxical twist. Here too he capped

[26] That impression cannot in the nature of things be documented; but it is
confirmed by simple comparison with II.

[27] A good example of his pugnacity, of his elenchic *persona*, may be found in
II. 23.

[28] See, e.g., II. 43.

Hecataeus.[29] Whether Herodotus derived the kernel of the Proteus story from someone else or, in effect, made it up himself, the story is a clever piece of rationalistic criticism at once ironic and amusing. The old man of the sea, now a king of Egypt, is angered by Menelaus because of his sacrifice of two of Proteus' subjects, this being, evidently, a rationalization of *Odyssey* IV. 351ff. Stesichorus' *eidolon* is whisked out of its insubstantial existence; Helen is sent to Egypt and nothing to Troy. Still Troy was destroyed. The paradoxical flavour and wit of the story is perspicuous, and its intended effect upon an audience less interested in *Quellenkritik* than we are need not be doubted. Somewhat similar in sensationalistic intent, though more subdued because of its very nature, is his account of Egyptian history. He narrates the actions of the more memorable Pharaohs without any evident direction. The monuments of their rule—Sanacharib's statue (141), Rhodopis' pyramid (134)—are calculated to impress and entertain. It is striking that there is no hint of that vision of humanity defining his work as a whole and prevalent, especially, in I and VII–IX. There is nothing here of *hybris*, of the effects of prosperity, of the importance of liberty.[30] Rhampsinitus' thief (121), Mycerinus (129ff.), even the

[29] Hecataeus' rationalization of Egyptian place names (see *FGrHist* 1, Ff. 307–9) is as prosaic as his justification of Menelaus. Herodotus' version is more imaginative and, from the point of view of the Greek audience, more startling, because it imputes impiety to Menelaus (II. 118f.). Herodotus apparently took pleasure in treating the exalted heroes of Homer cynically—compare the judgement implicit in I. 4. Thus he outdid Hecataeus in being unsentimental as well as realistic. Calling Herodotus' version 'anti-Greek' (Jacoby, in his commentary, among others) because of the tart handling of Menelaus overstates it considerably. It discerns weighty objects where no more need be assumed than objectivity and humour. Herodotus liked the story and adopted it or adapted it because he thought his audience also would. Von Fritz's assertion, op. cit., p. 106, that 'every sentence of the story shows it to be genuine Egyptian' is incomprehensible to me. As to its source, it is easier to believe that the story arose out of Herodotus' imaginative questions put to the priests than that some Greco-Egyptian with a similar flair duplicated Herodotus. Certainly the notion of some titanic propagandistic battle being fought out in Egypt, the issue being to exculpate or condemn the Homeric hero, should refute itself.

[30] Consider his treatment of Apries in II. 161; how in II. 133 the 'fated' decline of Egypt is mere window-dressing for a story about Mycerinus.

thoroughly bad Cheops (124ff.), point no moral lesson. They are vivid pictures presented for their own sake. History is 'pure', so to speak, in the sense that it is directionless; it is antiquarian. Its justification is that it exists and that it is intrinsically interesting, not that its events constitute a sequence, like the causes of the Persian Wars, needing to be traced because of the importance of what its march involves. This, above all, explains why speeches or, rather, the kind of speech expressive of Herodotus' didactic purposes, are missing.[31] There are places where we might expect them.[32] Even were there not, Herodotus might have invented them— would have invented them, one may say, if when he wrote about Egypt he had already become possessed of that philosophy dominating his vision of life. But Herodotus here is not didactic in any profound way. Book II was written to instruct and entertain.[33] It reveals Herodotus' basic interest in history and his natural inclination to research, the making of inquiries. But it is the work of a younger man not yet in control of the techniques or in possession of the mental attitudes of the author of Book I.

The change in Herodotus' technique from such a book as II to the immeasurably more complex portions of his history as, especially, I and VII–IX, is the mark of an increasingly mature and practised style. More especially, however, it denotes also a shift in intentions and a new conception of his role. In Book II Herodotus presented the record as he saw or heard it. He was careful to indicate his sources and to make it clear when he spoke in his own right.[34] His purpose was to

---

[31] See A. Deffner, *Die Rede bei Herodot und ihre Weiterbildung bei Thukydides* (Diss. München 1933), pp. 11f. The distinction is between the type of speech furthering action and that which conveys a deeper meaning.

[32] Deffner, p. 41, observed that he might well have employed one for Rhampsinitis in II. 121.

[33] Perhaps Herodotus' recognition of the comparatively light ends he is serving—the delectation of his audience—rather than his 'deeply religious nature' keeps him from speaking about sacred subjects in II. Thus in II. 170 he asserts that he does not consider it proper to give the names of the graves in Sais ἐπὶ τοιούτῳ πρήγματι. The qualification may be significant.

[34] He disclaims reponsibility for what he relates in II. 123, 130, 146; IV. 96,

reproduce whatever he could find of interest, his chief responsibility being fidelity to the record.[35] There is no principle of exclusion on the grounds of unlikelihood; the march of the narrative is subordinate to the tales that can be told. Omnipresent as Herodotus is as the reporter, his art is, in comparison to what it will become, essentially journalistic: he adopts or reproduces his sources in immediate dependence upon them without that *Vertieferung* which elsewhere is his hallmark. Though that fidelity to the tradition remains with him throughout his career, other devices of a very different order have become superimposed upon it and Herodotus becomes more than the faithful reporter of fact and tradition. That change is signalled by his resort to the 'adviser motif'[36] and to a new type of speech permitting him to clarify and point the issues. The latter, especially, was a momentous invention and it is not the less startling because speeches already served a similar purpose in epic poetry. In taking these expedients for granted as we seem to have done, being rather more concerned with analysing their use and hunting for earlier parallels, we perhaps forget that they were neither normal nor predictable developments. For there is a wide gulf between even the imaginative expounder of the traditions and habits of foreign peoples and the author of devices of this nature. They are fictional. With their introduction by Herodotus, 'history' acquired a poetic and philosophical dimension that, transmuting its character, raised it to the higher imaginative level we associate with the

---

173, 187, 191, 195; VI. 82, 137; VII. 152. It is noteworthy that only one such disclaimer appears in VII–IX. Furthermore, the remark in VII. 152, like that of VI. 82 and VI. 137, reflects his caution in crediting statements that are apparently tendentious. That marks them off from the kind of hedge made in II and IV. Those in II and IV are intended to make his audience aware that his own credulity is not to be gauged by what he relates. The later instances— VI. 82, 137; VII. 152—proceed from Herodotus' desire to have the audience judge cautiously of what he tells them. The difference is symptomatic of his own different stance.

[35] The difference in tone between II.99 and I.6ff. is instructive. In both cases Herodotus is presenting 'history'. In II he is no more than middleman; in Book I he is magisterial.

[36] See R. Lattimore, *Classical Philology* 34 (1939), 24ff.

drama. For these devices were not adopted to round a picture or give verisimilitude. Nor are they a mere extension of the so-called Ionian novelistic. They permit a utilization for philosophical and moral purposes of what is except for the mind of the historian a neutral record. Herodotus, in adopting these devices, was moved with new purpose transcending that of 'traditional' logography and that initial stage of his own as exemplified in II. Herodotus became a creative artist with the intention of working on the minds and emotions of his audience. He injected into the record of Persian, Lydian, and Greek history an importance reaching beyond the facts in themselves. History became moral and Herodotus didactic.

The presence, therefore, in Herodotus' *Histories* of such a book as II provides all the evidence that is necessary to show his progression from something like a conventional historian concerned to give a broad picture of the political, intellectual, religious, and social life of a people into an artist imaginatively harnessing this material to higher purposes. Interest in the extraordinary, in the culture and history of foreign countries, and the desire to write about them seem to have been the original impulses which set him on his travels.

Such a picture of Herodotus as this, I suggest, is in keeping with the literary scene of which he was a part and allows sufficiently for his own innate originality and historical and ethnographical interest, on the one hand, and for the fluidity of 'logography' on the other. It is in accord, also, with what we ordinarily might have expected, judging from Herodotus' final work, to have occupied his 'apprenticeship'. His account of Egypt is the kind of work resulting from the kind of travel that was the precondition of the complex and world-wise masterpiece that crowned his labours.

II

THE PERSIAN EMPIRE

HERODOTUS' literary activity in the years that intervened between the work on Egypt and his occupation with the Persian History, which provides a clear signpost of his intellectual development, cannot be determined with certainty. The series of ethnographies (whether or not they were an intrinsic part of the *Persica*) cannot be dated firmly in their relative order. For unless Herodotus is supposed to have written the *Histories* in one draft from end to end, only uncertainty can be promoted by attempting to infer temporal priorities from the present system of cross-references in his work. There is, for instance, no need to suppose, from II. 7. 1, that Herodotus had been to Athens before he visited Egypt; or to assume, with J. E. Powell,[1] from II. 104. 1, which points to similarity between the Colchians and the Egyptians, that Herodotus made two Egyptian journeys, one before, and one after, his visit to Scythia; or to conclude, with von Fritz,[2] from the same evidence, that Herodotus went first to Scythia and then (but once) to Egypt. These assumptions would be binding only if one chooses to believe that Herodotus did not emend his work in the process of preparing it for publication and that when he did so he was not already familiar with the burden of its contents. Yet the conclusion seems unavoidable that Herodotus, at the final stage (there probably were also several earlier ones) wrote out or read to a scribe from an earlier text what became the 'final draft'. If so, it is plain that, like any author, he would make deletions, additions, and changes

---

[1] *The History of Herodotus* (Cambridge, 1939), p. 25.
[2] *Die Griechische Geschichtschreibung*, I *Anmerkungen*, p. 90, n. 89.

with a view to any number of considerations; their effect will have been to obscure and confuse the order of composition.

But the point of central importance in charting the progress of Herodotus' intellectual advance is largely irrelevant to the dating of one ethnographical portion of his work relatively to another. The critical matter is that he advanced to write a Persian history which was revolutionary in conception. The author of the *Persikoi logoi* reveals by his choice of subject and by his treatment of it a marked and recognizable change in psychology and historical sense compared to what he had already achieved (as in the Egyptian *logos*) and to what had been foreshadowed or accomplished by his literary predecessors. The uniqueness of his approach has, however, been taken for granted, perhaps because it is nothing new to us. Perhaps, also, it is because our critical terminology is more effective in lumping works together than in marking off their intrinsic differences. Herodotus' was not the first *Persica*: was not the subject common? Since the same word is used to describe the work of Herodotus and those of others, it is easy enough from that point of view to assume that Herodotus' *logos* is one of a species and so explicable in terms of other authors or, more vaguely, of the 'times'.[3] But Herodotus wrote a different kind of *Persica*, a different kind of history, from what theretofore had been developed. That is clear from the work of his older colleague, Dionysius of Miletus.

The little that is known about Dionysius' *Persica* is enough to indicate, by contrast, Herodotus' momentous advance. Dionysius articulated his account of Persia by the life span of the kings whose *res gestae* he wrote.[4] The work must have been similar to the historical portion of Herodotus' account

---

[3] See, for example, Schmid-Stählin, *Griechischen Literaturgeschichte* I. 2. 584, who explain Herodotus' *Persica* as an attempt to 'enlarge, correct, and replace' the works of Dionysius of Miletus and Charon of Lampsacus. See Jacoby, *Abhandlungen*, p. 199, n. 80.

[4] That follows from the book-list in *FGrHist* 687, T 1, where one of the books of his *Persica* began as τὰ μετὰ Δαρεῖον. The principle of organization was the lives of the kings, not what we find in Herodotus.

of Egypt—a discussion of the ruling kings and, in the framework of that, their memorable deeds. That fact alone is suggestive: it indicates that the level of narrative found in Book II was typical of 'historical writing' for Herodotus and for his colleagues—until Herodotus himself transcended it. For the *Persica* is history with a direction. Unlike the history of Egypt and Dionysius' account of Persia, the subject—in this case the countries tributary to Persia—is subordinate to a truly historical principle: 'the means by which the Persians took control of Asia' (I. 95).

The difference is important because Herodotus' *Persica* implies the utilization of a thematic conception of history. The material which is the subject of narration is coerced into an historical pattern. The focus is no longer the *res gestae* of a series of kings. Herodotus' story hinges on the progressive domination by Persia first of all Asia and then of a part of Europe. The various rulers rise and fall but all lead the same march of Persia; *that* aspect of their rule makes them important. Thus, although Dionysius related essentially the same material, probably in the manner of Charon of Lampsacus[5] and Herodotus in II, the principles by which each organized it diverged, Herodotus having come to utilize it on a higher plane. Herodotus made Persian conquest, a historical development, the principle threading together the subjects of the *Persica*. By so doing, he created history with direction, with meaning. Teleological, not antiquarian in focus, the *Persica* is a causative history involving the subordination and explanation of the *erga* which, formerly, it was enough merely to describe. This is a new element in 'historical' writing of decisive importance to the development of that genre.[6]

[5] See Chapter I, n. 25.

[6] Herodotus' theme may be commonplace to us but there is no perceptible foundation for the view that 'In the Greek motherland the thought of ancestral enmity between Greeks and Asiatics, which Hecataeus had already expressed, first acquired its living force through the campaigns of Darius and Xerxes' (K. F. Pagel, *Die Bedeutung des aitiologischen Momentes für Herodots Geschichtsschreibung* [Diss. Berlin 1927], p. 13). That theme cannot be attributed to

Herodotus' evolution from an historian of the traditional type, the narrator of things as they happened, into one who accommodated these things to an historical pattern of his own creation, is not self-explanatory. It required conceptual genius, evident as it may be to us after more than two thousand years of habituation to the concept. The step was essential in that gradual process by which the Greeks 'discovered' the kind of historical writing which from that time became an important facet in the manner of thought of the western world.

Gaetano De Sanctis recognized that the Persian History is the link between the ethnographies on the one hand and the monograph of Xerxes' War on the other.[7] It seemed to him to explain some of the problematical features of the *Histories*. He argued that although the ethnographies are badly explained even as digressions in the history of the struggle between Greek and barbarian (and this he defined as the primary theme of the work as a whole), such narratives as that in Book II, the Lydian *logos*, and others can satisfactorily be explained by way of the *Persica*.[8] Similarly, Friederich Focke[9] observed that the Persian *logos* is marked

Hecataeus on the strength of Hdt. VI. 137. 2, and it was also unknown to the dramatists until the production of Euripides' *Helen*. Many scholars see the antinomy as self-evident. But the panoramic view which must be the prerequisite of the conception of such a theme cannot be prior to or detached from the accumulation of the kind of detailed historical knowledge which Herodotus was the first to systematize. Many a Greek, including Hecataeus (Hdt. V. 36. 2) knew the extent of Persia's empire. That no more implies the theme of 'imperialism' than Xerxes' War an ancestral enmity. The great Persian War is only the culmination of Persian imperialism because Herodotus acquired the perspective to see it in that fashion.

[7] *Studi di storia della storiografia greca, Il pensiero storico* 34 (Firenze, 1951), 25f.

[8] De Sanctis, p. 23, limited himself to giving reasons why the *logoi* need not have been initially independent. He argued that the organic and artistic unity of Book II and other *logoi* as they stand do not prove their 'original absolute independence'. These, the 'more salient' parts of his history, acquired these traits because they were given as lectures. That, however, would explain why Herodotus' lectures, which we do not have, were unified and self-consistent. It does not explain why the work from which, on this hypothesis, he cut them out presents them also as organic and artistic wholes. De Sanctis has Herodotus' lectures moulding the grander design he believes to have been anterior to them.

[9] *Herodot als Historiker*, pp. 43f.

off from the other *logoi* by its theme; since it cannot be ranged beside the others but rather 'subsumes' them it was conceptually prior to them. Hence, in his view, 'the present disposition of the work was planned from the beginning.'

There is every reason to agree with these scholars in so far as they conceive of the Persian History as a frame for the ethnographies—i.e., that the ethnographies are introduced by way of the Persian conquest of the lands described. The one exception is the Lydian *logos*, but this is easily explained.[10] The idea, then, of Persian conquest explains the principle according to which the ethnographies are disposed throughout the *Persica*. But does this also suggest, as Focke inferred, that the principle of organization was conceptually prior to the coalescence of the material structured by it? The deduction does not seem cogent. Disquisitions on Egypt, Libya, Scythia, etc., the treatment of a specific land as a subject or topic in itself, are not implicit in the theme of Persian expansion. Perhaps it would be clearer to say that anyone motivated by the idea of writing about Persian expansion would by that definition of his aim limit himself more or less to what was relevant to that theme. A major ethnographical study of the countries reduced to submission implies a different motivation—quite obviously, the desire to write about those countries. The desire to describe 'the manner in which the Persians conquered Asia' (I. 95) implies that the discussion will turn on the motives prompting Persia to advance and the means by which she accomplished her objective. A description of the people subjected is certainly entailed. But a discussion of the conquered people, a thorough study, for example, of the fauna of Egypt, *introduced* by a statement of the motives and means of conquest is palpably different.

The problem is partly one of definition. Certain conclusions are drawn not so much from strict observation of the subject matter in which Herodotus, by lingering, reveals his interest as from possible logical conclusions permitted by *our*

[10] See De Sanctis, op. cit., p. 25.

definition of the *Persica*. If we say that the 'basic theme' is Persian Imperialism or Persian Expansion it is easy from that point to argue that the rest is implicit—if that be defined crisply as 'the people that were subjugated'. But *is* Herodotus' subject the 'Persian Conquest' or is it rather 'the histories, customs, and marvels of the peoples absorbed into the Persian Empire'? If it is the former, the 'ethnographies' require explanation. If the latter, the introduction of the idea of Persian conquest, hardly implied in the ethnographies, needs accounting for. But what of Herodotus' own words? He said that his description will be of the 'manner in which the Persians gained the hegemony over Asia.' The answer must be that although such a definition is compatible with what he wrote, it is also misleading enough to be demonstrably inappropriate. For his description of that conquest is perfunctory, however important the idea of that conquest is as an organizing principle.

It is commonly stated that the *Persica* stamps Herodotus as the historian of Persian imperialism and, alternately, as the historian of the Persian empire. That these two descriptions are used as if equivalent indicates how easily related but different ideas can be merged together. The difference is important. The theme of imperialism, the psychological probing of the drive to conquest, is as absent in the *Persica* as it is prominent and central in VII–IX. That theme should not be interpolated into the earlier books because the same man wrote all of them. Herodotus' succinct description of the extension of Persia implies the remorseless advance of that power and testifies to 'imperialism'. But only by semantical legerdemain can an implication be denominated as the 'subject' to which Herodotus addressed himself.

Herodotus' description of the impulse to conquest is minimal in the *Persica*. The reasons prompting the attacks of Cyrus, Cambyses, and Darius are specific; it would be an exaggeration to say that they are even discussed. Their purpose in the *Persica* is pragmatic. They are provided to justify an action, not adduced as if they were thematically interrelated. So momentous a project as attacking Greece can be lightly prompted and as lightly considered because of the desire of a Crotoniate physician to escape from Persia (III. 131ff.).

Instead of those eternal laws prompting the expansion of states, leading rulers on to a path of conquest—the theme so important in VII–IX—what in fact do we find in the *Persica*? Cyrus marched on Babylon (I. 178. 1) because he did. Cyrus 'desired' to attack the Massagetae (I. 201) because of his birth and his good fortune (I. 204. 2). Xerxes' motives in VII may ultimately rest on comparable considerations: what matters is that there they are explicit and fundamental. Cambyses 'made a campaign against Egypt' (II. 1); a reason is given in III. 1. The inexorable march of Persia may be implicit in the idea that Cambyses conquered Egypt out of anger induced by a deception practised upon him by King Amasis. But it is not presented in that light. Cambyses 'wanted' to conquer Ethiopia (III. 17). Darius advanced on Scythia because he 'wanted revenge' for something remote in the past (IV. 1). Pity for Pheretime leads Artaunes to launch an invasion of Libya (IV. 165–7). The fact that all these pragmatic explanations, some defined, others left vague, can be taken together as individual examples of the same phenomenon, Persian imperialism, merely shows that we have the capacity to generalize from particulars. Herodotus' text does not substantiate the opinion that he did the same. The 'idea' of conquest, the subject of Persian imperialism, follows from our definition of the *Persica*, not his own. It is difficult, therefore, to see how the statement he made about describing 'the manner in which Persia gained the hegemony' can be taken as a definition of his initial intentions; we should not over-intellectualize that statement since Herodotus did not do so.

Herodotus has indeed made a pattern out of the assortment of facts under his command—the pattern of Persia's advance, a series of conquests seen as a single movement. But he has not yet attempted to probe the causes of the movement or made it his subject. This account of the Persian Empire is not the same as a history of Persian imperialism. Herodotus has not, until the latter part of it,[11] described an act of conquest or discussed the motives inducing it in any substantial way. It is no more his subject than Roman imperialism was Mommsen's in his *Provinces of the Roman Empire*. At the same time, there is no question that Herodotus has utilized the idea of Persian expansion in order to structure his work. But it is his *work* which is being structured. That principle explains his organization of the ethnographical material, not his purpose in having collected it in the first place. And although Herodotus' definition of a proper history of Persia might theoretically have required discussion of the nature and site, the laws, marvels, and history of any place absorbed or attacked by the Persian giant, it should be apparent, in that case, that he was not motivated to write a history of Persia or its expansion. If Herodotus had set out to do so, as Focke believed, the emphasis of his account could not so fundamentally have been inverted. Focke was quick to take exception to the idea that Herodotus could have written 'geographies' simultaneously with the *Persica*.[12] He is not freed from a comparable dilemma merely by defining such a work as Book II as 'historical'.[13]

Herodotus' main emphasis, the substance of his narrative, must be the guide to his predominating interests. To speak of 'themes' as if they were all equal in weight is to stray from an empirical observation of the text, where the clues are to be sought. For one very interesting feature of the *Persica* (I–VI) is that it betrays a suggestive shift in Herodotus' direction and interests; it is not monolithic. Herodotus' description of the causes for conquest and his accounts of the conquests themselves became increasingly, though gradually,

[11] See below, p. 32.

[12] Op. cit., p. 45, n. 66.

[13] The difficulty was felt by Schmid-Stählin, *Griechische Literaturgeschichte* I. 2, who were forced to assume on page 562 (though not on page 584) that Herodotus' Egyptian journey was prior to his conception of the *Persica*.

elaborate as he progressed. The texture of his account under-
goes detectable change in Books IV and V. His absorbing
interest in ethnography is increasingly balanced in Book IV
(his description of the opposition of the Scyths to Darius)
with dramatic commentary on some of the issues raised by
Persia's advance (see, e.g., IV. 118, 127). From that point,
through the Ionian Revolt, to the battle at Marathon, the
theme of Persian expansion is no longer peripheral but central in its own right. The development of the theme of
Persian expansion from an organizational principle into the
actual subject of the *Persica* suggests clearly that Herodotus
advanced from the simple to the complex—a shift already
indicated by the presence of ethnographical material which
cannot be explained satisfactorily by reference to that theme.
More specifically, it suggests that he may have been led to
the idea of Persian conquest as a result of his ethnographical
studies rather than the other way around. Is such an hypothesis reasonable?

Let us imagine that Herodotus continued on the course he
had set with the Egyptian *logos* and wrote other such narratives.
Let us further suppose that he determined to bind up all of
this material (that already committed to paper and that
which he foresaw) in a work which then would be a series of
ethnographical-historical studies about the chief foreign
countries of the civilized world. If he were so inspired, what
problems would have confronted him? Chiefly one, we may
imagine: that of organization. It might easily enough have
been solved by organizing them, as Jacoby supposed he
intended to do, in a *periodos ges*, a geographical work of
massive scale. The thought of proceeding in the fashion of
Hecataeus, though not blindly so, since his work would be
more solid and more various, might naturally have occurred
to him. It cannot be doubted that Hecataeus was a formative
influence on him and on any other Greek author intending
to relate to his countrymen something of the mysteries of the
peoples living beyond their borders. Such a book can easily
be imagined: one narrative after another, threaded together

on a geographical string—the Mediterranean coastline. In such a system, the history of each nation would be presented autonomously as the series of the more memorable deeds of each ruler.

If Herodotus had written a number of ethnographies it is clear that a striking phenomenon would have attracted his attention. Persia inevitably obtruded itself into the affairs of the Asiatic nations. Herodotus would in each case see that the people he was writing about had their historical development truncated by Persian conquest or arrested by Persian attack. This observation will have given him a concrete notion about 'Persian expansion' as a systematic manifestation of Persian power. Indeed, it is hard to see how the notion can have come to him prior to these particular observations. At that point, might not the idea of a book introducing these ethnographies by way of Persia have naturally occurred to him as an infinitely more interesting and less repetitious method of organization?

The idea of introducing a series of ethnographies at the point when Persia swallowed up or attacked the countries under discussion would of its own force have impelled Herodotus to become innovative. Although the historical portions of the other ethnographies could remain 'traditional', obviously the Persian *logos* must become less a subject in itself than a framework for all the others. Not the lives of the rulers but the record of their conquests must be presented in order to fulfil the purpose of introducing the ethnographies at the appropriate moment. His 'theme' was not the Persian conquest: his subject was the ethnographies, the Persian conquest a device. Initially he intended it to be no more than that.

Such a hypothesis as this at least has the virtue of explaining some of the problems the *Persica* presents. By insisting that his 'theme' originally was 'Persian expansion' his mechanical use of that idea as well as his attention to ethnography becomes hard to fathom. By recognizing it for what it is, its presence and the reasons for it can be inferred.

Is the word 'device' derogatory? Should our respect for his great conceptual advance blind us to the fact that such a 'digression' as II is motivated very mechanically? Arguments adduced to show that Book II and the other *logoi* are well integrated if we look beyond them to the higher themes subsuming them stem from misconceived piety. Herodotus does not need such justification; it is more important to recognize the great stride forward implied by Herodotus' subordination of his material to an historical concept.

The principle of Persian conquest initially supplied Herodotus with a means for the organization of his material. But as he progressed it is evident that the idea of such expansion became increasingly important to him. The process must have been gradual and tentative. First he baldly stated the motives for conquest. Specific details were given, such as pity for Pheretime or vengeance against the Scyth. And with this came also further inventions giving some substance to the idea of conquest. The speech of the King of the Ethiopians, for example, adds some depth to the meaning of the encounters between Persia and the states she wished to bring into subjection (III. 21. 2). But the idea of Persian conquest plainly acquired a life of its own bringing a shift in interest from ethnographical narration to the description of combat and resistance to conquest when he became involved in IV and the succeeding books. At this point the logic invoked to 'explain' Book II and the other *logoi* is cogent. From the Scythian campaign onward the Persian advance is no longer merely a bridge between subjects but explains the elaboration of what actually is discussed. The Ionian Revolt is Herodotus' proper subject; he is now involved in the portrayal of historical episodes vitally connected with the theme of Persian advance. Herodotus' statement of his intent as to describe 'the means by which Persia secured the hegemony of Asia' applies with full force.

One consequence of his dedication to this new theme was far-reaching. The new subject required a new method. A writer of ethnography, of τὰ λεγόμενα on any subject—a

writer who makes τὰ λεγόμενα his subject—is completely at
the mercy of his material. What he can discover he reports,
with his narrative being that report. What happens, though,
when a writer decides to cut his own swath through τὰ
λεγόμενα and pursue a subject of his own definition? The
problems are very different. If the subject is not just 'the
customs of the Scyths' but Darius' attack against them, if he
must describe the Ionian Revolt and not limit himself to an
allusion to that subjugation, history is viewed no longer
through the wrong end of the telescope. Although the mere
statement of a Persian advance was sufficient when a particular conquest was the bridge to conduct the reader to an
ethnographical study of the conquered people, now that the
conquest is the focal point of interest, the basis of Herodotus'
narrative, he must of course describe it. Herodotus began to
probe into matters in a way that slowed the race of events to a
standstill. And this required introducing into 'history' in
unprecedented fashion a richness of detail which until then
was purely the province of the epos.

The parallel is real, for Herodotus, not surprisingly,
borrowed some of his methods from Homer. What does
Herodotus' 'shift in interest' imply if not the desire on his
part to achieve something comparable to the *Iliad* in a work
of prose? Evidently, reflection on the material he had collected and familiarity with the idea of Persian conquest led
him to contemplate taking this gigantic step forward. For
gigantic it was, when we consider the utterly new realm into
which he stepped. He needed to become an *imaginative*
historian as well as the reporter of tradition.

The main facts he could discover. They were, nevertheless,
but facts. He would need to string them together and put
flesh on them if this prose work was to justify his ambition
and its novelty. Certainly he ferreted out all he could about
the actual circumstances from whatever source he could
track down. But he must amplify on his own. A discussion between advisers must be presented, not mentioned. If Histaeus is to be summoned home to Susa as a precondition of

the revolt of Ionia, Herodotus will now give us the words of
Megabazus (V. 23). The narrative is acted out as if it indeed were the epos. Now fateful decisions could be drama-
tized (IV. 133f.), the bearing of important figures watched
closely and their very words reported, with the result that
Histaeus, Aristagoras, Dionysius of Phocea, Miltiades,
Darius, and others, even collectives like Scyths and Ionians,
become 'real people'.

Herodotus turned to invention. He adapted the techniques
of the poets in order to give colour and life to an account
which by his own choice of subject absolutely required them.
History moved to the higher plane of imaginative recreation.
Once having accepted that principle as a part of his narrative
technique, Herodotus became an author of a different type
from what he had been. He could adopt for his own uses the
fictional devices of poetry. As he developed he exploited them
increasingly, as we can see from VII–IX, in order to make
his account not only vivid but also a means for presenting the
higher truths only fiction can convey.[14]

Herodotus' concern with ethnography, then, began as a
primary interest which led him to explore a more complex
possibility with fateful results. The ethnographical interest
was not a consequence of the more sophisticated theme he
eventually attempted. The idea of Persian expansion, though
initially conceived as the framework for the *logoi*, acquired
importance in its own right in virtue of Herodotus' expanding vision. In becoming the predominant theme of the
Persica, this concern to detail historical episodes and to impart
substance to them liberated Herodotus from the prosaic
sphere of his predecessors by making him an imaginative expounder of his material.

---

[14] The episodes involving Polycrates in III and Solon in I are instances of
Herodotus' method in its final perfection. The sharp contrast they present to
their surroundings is enough to indicate that they were created or polished when
Herodotus, at the peak of his powers, was absorbed in giving final shape to his
work as a whole. These episodes are the vehicle for a philosophy which nothing
else in these books suggests he attained to.

III

HERODOTUS AND ATHENS

HERODOTUS' *Histories* terminate with the collapse of Xerxes' effort against Greece in 479 B.C. This was the proper moment to end; it was the natural limit of the expansion of Persia which was his theme, and the beginning of the shrinking of her power.[1] As his project advanced, it naturally entailed (and explains) his inclusion of material about the Greeks themselves. The conquest of the Greeks in Ionia, the discussion of which must have been very far indeed from his thoughts when he made that voyage to Egypt, became now a necessary part of his narrative. From there it was a natural step to cross over to Europe with Datis and then with Xerxes. It is an interesting example of an idea generated for the sake of other considerations acquiring sufficient impetus of its own to become a guiding force. Herodotus, impelled by it, became a Greek historian as well as the historian of Persia. Just as Herodotus seized upon the idea of writing about Persian expansion in order to 'frame' the independently conceived ethnographies and found his interests and techniques diverted by the new conception, so did the concept of Persian expansion lead him to culminate the whole with a monograph on the Great War to which even the concept of Persian expansion became secondary.

An account of Xerxes' advance and repulse was implicit in the theme of Persian expansion. But the way he has written these books inescapably suggests, by the shift in emphasis

---

[1] Even if the *Histories* are unfinished (which I do not believe), the manner of his close is not a sign of it. The various arguments adduced to show that he should have continued to a later point, whether the capture of Byzantium, the founding of the Athenian league or even the death of Xerxes, are unnecessary in view of the aptness of the end he has made.

they reveal, that the theme of Persian imperialism was the occasion and not the cause of the monograph. VII–IX is a 'book' in itself, complete with *proœmium*; it has a beginning, middle and end testifying to its conceptual independence. It can even be separated from what precedes without contextual damage. What matters more is that Herodotus' focus is on the war itself: the theme of the expansion of Persia becomes a secondary consideration yielding in importance to themes directly intrinsic to the conflict described. More concretely, the nature of the opponents, the internal affairs of the Greeks, the issue of whether or not to fight—these are centrally thematic. War itself is the subject where before it was only the necessary link between the more important question (as he then viewed it) of the motivation for Persian attack and the nature of the country attacked and conquered. If one were to object that this is an inevitable consequence of Herodotus' decision to narrate the war, the answer surely is that the kind of description he has given us is not a consequence of that decision. The richness of the texture of VII–IX makes by comparison even such an account as the Ionian Revolt or the battle at Marathon seem perfunctory and jejune. Not the results or the causes of the war—though these are important components—but the mentality of the Greeks, individually and collectively, the factors uniting and dividing the Greek world, the dual leadership of Sparta and Athens, are the objects of Herodotus' direct concern. The presence of excursuses on Sparta and Athens scattered in prior books prepares us for the new emphasis. But can Herodotus have predicted that shift until he was led to make it? The decisive role exercised by these powers in the account of VII–IX he finally wrote, not his prevision of the treatment they would eventually receive, required that 'red thread' of Greek history winding its way from Books I to VII.[2] We may assume, at this stage, some revision of the *Persica* in order to

---

[2] Jacoby's phrase. I thus assume that the excursuses on Athenian and Spartan history were interpolated into his account during that final creative period when he was involved in writing VII–IX.

accommodate it to the final and now main section of the *Histories*.

The assumption that Herodotus revised the *Persica* in order to unify the whole in theme and tone seems preferable to the supposition that Herodotus both predicted and allowed for his own development. As I have tried to suggest, his growth is better to be understood as his response to progressively ambitious tasks. His development into the historian of the causes of man's actions rather than of actions achieved came out of his response to the problem of subordinating separate ethnographies, then his central interest, into a historical framework. From there his preoccupation with the theme of Persian imperialism is self-explanatory, and his decision to chronicle that ceaseless advance until finally it was checked is an unproblematic testimony to his imagination and to his industry. But the whole of VII–IX indicates a shift. What, then, induced him to become the historian of war?

The overriding philosophical and moral issues made explicit in his account of the conflict, the obvious importance which he attached to his narration—not as a 'prize composition' but as a serious document—excludes at once the possibility that he was an antiquarian responding to a public hunger for the fading details of that bygone day, an author in search of a congenial topic, the happy Herodotus reliving the joyful story of a Greek triumph. The result of the conflict assuredly was joyful to most Greeks. But can we so seriously misread Herodotus as to confound that joyful triumph with his account of the war? There is more to his monograph than the victories at Salamis and Mycale and the glorious defeat at Thermopylae. Herodotus did not like war and considered this one no better than any other.[3] Nor is his account of the Greek states sentimental or nostalgic. We underplay this because it is easy to think of the high points and easier still to compress the whole monograph into an affirmative message. But the message is affirmative because from our point of view the war was a success, not because

[3] VI. 98. 2.

Herodotus' message was affirmative. That is even clear in Pohlenz's statement that Herodotus wrote this work out of the 'proud and thankful feeling that the small and not even united Hellenic nation was capable of turning away the attack' of Persia.[4] But these words are false as to emphasis. 'Not even united' were better expressed as 'disunited'; *that* theme is more evident in Herodotus than his proud and thankful spirit.

Pohlenz's explanation of why Herodotus wrote VII–IX is fallacious not only because it sentimentalizes where Herodotus did not. It is methodologically wrong to detach Herodotus from his own historical context and make him respond directly to the very phenomenon he has described or, rather, to *his* description of that phenomenon. In 431 B.C. the gratitude of which Pohlenz speaks had lost its living force. Not even an epigram, much less a history, could be composed at that time in authentic response to such a feeling.

As the point is important, especially for the understanding of Herodotus—since explanations of this type have so frequently been invoked to explain why he wrote what he did—let us consider for a moment what is involved. To us the interval between 479 and 431 is a mere moment and so Pohlenz's type of explanation seems plausible. But who of us today would dream of similarly explaining the treatment of a given subject by a contemporary in terms of a reaction he possibly experienced fifty years ago? If today a middle-aged Frenchman wrote a history of World War I, would we explain it by his reaction to World War I? We could not do it because automatically we would realize that men live in their present and not in the past. We would assume, in the case of the supposititious Frenchman, that his interest in that war was crystallized by subsequent and contemporary events; we would, of a certainty, assume that he went back to the past driven by present considerations.[5] Yet Herodotus is supposed to have been 'thankful' in some active way, relieved as

4 Pohlenz, *Herodot*, p. 175.
5 Naturally I am not speaking of a professional academic.

Aeschylus may well have been. In this respect it is difficult to find a parallel to our treatment of Herodotus. Every other author is seen as responding to the conditions of his own time—i.e., the time in which he actually is writing. But Herodotus is interpreted as if he were motivated directly by the subject of his choice. The fallacy could not be more distortive of his intent and aims.

The question, then, is why Herodotus wrote this particular account of Xerxes' War. And the answer, if it be that he was grateful or proud, is satisfactory only if we realize that this gratitude and pride must have its source in something other than the Persian War: if he was grateful, let us say, it must be because events in his own time made him so. That correlation is as necessary for Herodotus as for any other author. His attitude to his subject, the emotions it raised in him, the emotions and attitudes he wished to convey to his audience, were contemporary attitudes, present emotions. His description of the Persian War is their vehicle, not their explanation.

In seeking to find some of the reasons prompting Herodotus to write VII–IX, therefore, we must attempt to understand the work as his response to contemporary conditions, and try to intepret from his work the likely stimuli to which, in part at least, it was a response. It need hardly be said that the complexity of any human being precludes assigning any single cause to a given act and that with an author, of all people, a variety of factors are contributary. But that does not suggest that we are wrong in seeking to isolate the political or philosophical factor in this particular instance, especially since the work is so heavily moral and political.[6] Eduard Meyer saw this clearly.[7] To him it was axiomatic that history was not written by the great historians *sine studio et ira*. Unlike some later critics, who seem almost to suppose that the greatness of Herodotus' work is but the reflection of

[6] Regenbogen, *Die Antike* 6 (1930), 226, 235f., emphasizes his 'metaphysical motivation,' but the two must interrelate.

[7] *Forschungen zur alten Geschichte* (Halle, 1899) II. 196ff.

the brilliance of the epoch he described, Meyer understood that the *Histories* must be the result of Herodotus' intense involvement in the contemporary world. No work of feeling can be divorced from the immediate and profound reactions of its creator. Hence Meyer propounded a theory of the genesis of the final version of the history rooting it solidly in the political situation of Herodotus' time—about 431 B.C. He argued that Herodotus became the partisan of Pericles and of Athens when the Peloponnesian War broke out. 'It seems evident to me,' he asserted, 'that Herodotus wrote as a defender of Athens and of her policies, as they were guided by Pericles, which led to the Peloponnesian War.'[8]

It would be fair to say that, with very few exceptions,[9] Meyer's interpretation of the *animus* of Herodotus has not so much been rejected as modified and rendered less abrasive. Modification, at the least, was necessary. Herodotus' work reveals a man to whom the prospect of the Peloponnesian War and the necessity of choosing sides in it would have been painful. The very breadth of his sympathies at once for Sparta and for Athens should effectively preclude the assumption that he could have been a proponent of Periclean politics in 431 B.C.; as Otto Regenbogen succinctly stated, his attitudes towards the other Greek states are not dictated by Athenian sympathies and antipathies.[10] Something of the uncompromising harshness of Meyer's hypothesis, consequently, was smoothed by later writers and, in Jacoby's treatment of the question, it became authoritative. For the year 431 B.C. Jacoby substituted 445; Herodotus became the exponent of Athens rather than of Pericles. 'Unconsciously at best did he defend Pericles' policies, in so far as Pericles and Athens were the same (*identische Grössen*). But it was the policies of the years from 460, not that of the '30's.'[11] Herodotus wrote as the 'proclaimer of Athenian fame. It was

[8] Ibid., 198.

[9] Regenbogen, loc. cit., p. 225, and, above all, H. Strasburger, *Historia* 4 (1955), 1–25.

[10] Regenbogen, loc. cit., p. 225.

[11] *RE Suppl.* II. 359. 43–7.

not that he wished to defend the politics of Pericles but rather he wanted to portray the services to Hellas of the state now guided by Pericles in a time when no one wished to hear anything about these services.'[12]

Although this statement of Herodotus' intent avoids the fatal objections implicit in the position taken by Meyer, the expedient is nevertheless unsatisfactory. It is, in fact, built upon illegitimate distinctions. The dichotomy made by Jacoby between Pericles and 'the state' is unreal. To say that Herodotus wished to describe the services of a state 'presently led by Pericles' is certainly to suggest that the connection between the state and its leadership by Pericles is accidental or comparatively unimportant. The implication is that the current policies of the state Herodotus wished to defend were somehow irrelevant. Jacoby has made Herodotus the defender of an abstraction. But Herodotus cannot have been induced to defend Athens except out of his regard for the city as he knew it. That was no abstraction but the active and energetic Athens of Pericles. Equally invalid is the suggestion that Herodotus could have wished to defend the Athens of the fifties and forties. Again Herodotus is ripped from his historical context. He did not publish his work in the fifties; if it were in fact a defence it would have been understood as a defence of Athens' involvement in the Archidamian War and Herodotus would not only have expected this but intended it. Are we really to suppose that he revised (or wrote) his work in the early years of the Archidamian War (as Jacoby admits) in order to present to his contemporaries a defence of Athens in the *forties*? That is impossible, whatever one's date for his having written the bulk of VII–IX.[13] It is an argument equivalent to that which

[12] Ibid., 359. 58–64.

[13] The date of his revision, if it was that, is well within the Archidamian War. Indeed, on the strength of VI. 98. 2, which suggests a date after 424 B.C., VII. 235. 2, which suggests 424 (cf. Thuc. IV. 55), and IX. 73. 3, which suggests sometime after 421, he was still occupied with his history after the end of the Archidamian War—which explains why Aristophanes parodied him in *Birds* 1124ff. But I argue this matter elsewhere.

will have Herodotus 'defending' the Athens of 480 B.C. If the Athens of 480 B.C. was denigrated, if one wished to hear nothing about Athens' prior services to Hellas, it was because of hostility to contemporary Athens. In this context of polemic and distrust, of the division of all Greece into two camps, a defender of Athenian fame was a defender of Athens. The object of Herodotus' alleged justification cannot be retrojected to an earlier time, whether it be 445 B.C. or 480. If, in a time when war was all but inevitable or actually had broken out, Herodotus was incited to write these books (or revise them) 'inspired by a sincere admiration and a desire to contribute to her glory',[14] he cannot but have been the exponent of the regime then under attack, and a very zealous one since his motive for writing was actually exculpatory. There cannot, I think, be any compromise about this.[15] Those who wish to believe that Herodotus was inspired to write this history in order to contribute to the glory of Athens by reminding her critics of that noble achievement must be prepared to admit that Herodotus intended his defence to be a justification of Periclean Athens and of the policies pursued by that state before and during the Archidamian War.

Certainly there can be no doubt that the political conditions of his own time were decisive in making Herodotus treat of the Persian War in the manner that he has. He wrote a detailed and psychologically rich study centring on the two states, Sparta and Athens, which then were allies but now at each other's throat. He was not writing in isolation about 'ancient history' or unwinding a thread that was

---

[14] Powell, *The History of Herodotus*, p. 81; cf. p. 88.

[15] Such, for example, as that adopted by R. Walzer, *Gnomon* 6 (1930): 'Certainly it is unjustified to make Herodotus a conscious adherent of Periclean policies and his work a kind of political pamphlet for the goals of an Athenian party' (p. 579). Herodotus has a special preference for the Alcmeonids 'although one should deny a partiality to the policy of Pericles and his party' (p. 582). Herodotus' judgement of Athens in VII. 139 involves his own awareness that he was stamping himself before the world as pro-Athenian—'a significantly positive position although irrelevant to contemporary politics (*wenn auch nicht tagespolitischen Sinn*)' (p. 583).

severed in 479 B.C. He was writing a book at a time when these two states were locked in combat and he was directing it to an audience less capable than we of arbitrary dissociation and which would of a certainty have extrapolated conclusions of immediate moment, as Herodotus well knew, from his account. To this extent, at least, Eduard Meyer's belief that Herodotus cannot be understood except with reference to the contemporary political scene is realistic and plausible. The objection, simply, is that Meyer's emphasis on one aspect of Herodotus' sympathies has produced an unbalanced and distorted picture of the man and a narrow and partial statement of his intent.

On the positive side, there can be no doubt that Herodotus admired the city of the violet crown. One of his most emphatic remarks expressed in what for him is a singular manner registers his appreciation of the decisive role of the Athenians in the conflict. 'And here I feel constrained to deliver an opinion, which most men, I know, will dislike, but which, as it seems to me to be true, I am determined not to withhold. Had the Athenians, from fear of the approaching danger, quitted their country, or had they without quitting it submitted to the power of Xerxes, there would certainly have been no attempt to resist the Persians by sea; in which case, the course of events by land would have been the following. Though the Peloponnesians might have carried ever so many breastworks across the Isthmus, yet their allies would have fallen off from the Lacedaemonians, not by voluntary desertion, but because town after town must have been taken by the fleet of the barbarians; and so the Lacedaemonians would at last have stood alone, and, standing alone, would have displayed prodigies of valour, and died nobly. Either they would have done thus, or else, before it came to that extremity, seeing one Greek state after another embrace the cause of the Medes, they would have come to terms with King Xerxes; and thus, either way Greece would have been brought under Persia. . . . If then a man should now say that the Athenians were the saviours of Greece, he would not exceed the truth. For they truly held the scales, and whichever side they espoused must have carried the day.'[16]

But it is a far step from the recognition of Herodotus' admiration of Athenian valour in 480 B.C. (or, rather, realization of their decisive importance) and his recognition that they 'turned the scales' to the conclusion that his history was born out of an attempt to justify Athenian policies in the contemporary world. That Herodotus felt compelled to state what he realized would for his audience be an unpleasant truth proves beyond doubt that Herodotus was persuaded of the magnitude of the Athenian contribution. But that opinion is an inevitable indication of his political standpoint only if it be presumed that Herodotus, if he were not a partisan of Athens, must have been her enemy. The fact that Athenian loyalists will have agreed with him does not necessarily make him an Athenian loyalist. This passage is capable of at least two constructions: that he was a partisan of Athens is one, that he was truthful and no enemy is another. To determine which of the two is more likely to be correct more evidence than this is certainly needed.

The work as a whole does not read like a justification of Athens. If that was his intent, the manner in which he has effected it is exceedingly odd. For had Herodotus been driven to defend Athens before her critics, one would think that he would have written a work to secure that objective. Has the question really been asked whether this work would have produced any such effect? Would even VII. 139 contribute to that end? One effect of his history on us, moderns already enamoured of Athens, is to fortify the conviction of Athenian greatness. Yet I doubt that even a modern reader would seek to defend the Athens of Pericles by way of Herodotus' *Histories*. And what of Herodotus' own audience, the negatively disposed observer?[17] Would he, on reading the passage

[16] Hdt. VII. 139; Rawlinson's translation.

[17] Even the Athenians failed to understand the work as an encomium: see Schmid-Stählin, *Griechische Literaturgeschichte* I. 2, p. 664. It would be unwise to build on the alleged gift to Herodotus reported by Diyllus (*FGrHist* 73, F 3). Ten talents are far too many. More important, the gift is unnoticed by Isocrates

quoted above, take a milder view towards Pericles? In order
for him to do so, Herodotus would have had to point his
account correspondingly. Since it is obvious that he has not
done so, the possibility exists that we have confounded our
reaction to a scattering of passages with his motivation for
having written them.

The Athenians, it is true, were themselves quick to justify
their empire by pointing to earlier exploits.[18] But unless that
connection be made explicit it is unsubstantial, especially so
for Herodotus, to whom such a justification would be
meaningless. Prior successes do not justify; they explain what
nevertheless may be unjustifiable. The kind of reasoning
adopted by the Thucydidean ambassadors of Athens to
Sparta is alien to Herodotus' mentality. Our action in the
Persian War, they say, explains how we grasped the empire. 'And the nature of the case first compelled us to
advance our empire to its present height; fear being our
principal motive, though honour and interest afterwards
came in. And at last, when almost all hated us, when some
had already revolted and had been subdued, when you had
ceased to be the friends that you once were, and had become
objects of suspicion and dislike, it appeared no longer safe to
give up our empire; especially as all who left us would fall to
you.' This realistic but amoral argument presupposes a
different set of values from those of Herodotus. Thucydides'
explicit defence of the empire as a natural consequence of the
Athenian contribution of 480–79 B.C. cannot justifiably be
projected into the mind and history of Herodotus.[19] The
Thucydidean argument invokes a standard of justification
and explanation of man's conduct inimical to Herodotus'
more traditional view. Clearly neither the empire nor the

---

in *Antidosis* 166. If the *datum* of Eusebius (Hier. Ol. 83,4; 445/4 B.C.) is connected,
then the tradition is certainly spurious. But speculation is vain. See Jacoby, *RE
Suppl.* II. 229. 12–18.

[18] Thuc. I. 73f. The translation which follows is Crawley's.
[19] Cf. Regenbogen, loc. cit., p. 225.

course set by Pericles are by implication justified in the *Histories*.

Two interlocking assumptions each used to support the other, which then lend their cumulative weight to prop up the thesis that Herodotus defended Athens, are that Herodotus was a 'Periclean' and an admirer of the Athenian democracy. To the extent that both are inferences from the emphatic passage already quoted (VII. 139), the argument is circular. Beyond that, however, there seems to be little more than that predisposition in the minds of most of us to attribute orthodox opinions to the great historian. But we do so at the risk of misreading Herodotus. Much, for example, is made of V. 78, which has even been called Herodotus' 'formal political credo'.[20] Here, after his description of the successful repulse by the Athenians of her enemies shortly after the overthrow of the tyranny in 510 B.C., Herodotus continued as follows: 'not in one respect alone, but in general, does *isegoria* show itself to be a thing worth taking seriously if even the Athenians, when they were ruled by tyrants, were superior to none of their neighbours in war, but, being repressed, were deliberately cowardly. When they gained their freedom, every man of them became the more zealous to achieve for himself.'

That this is praise of democracy *qua* democracy is not obvious. It certainly does not follow that the democratic way was his preference above all others.[21] For Herodotus' approval of *isegoria* is not an endorsement, even by implication, of one government against another. The basic distinction he intended is clear from the text. The antithesis is between freedom and despotism, and democracy is secondary to it. ἐλευθερωθέντων is the key word; the quality of *eleutheria* rather than the intrinsic nature of democracy, as a specific form of government, is the issue. The passage as it stands is compatible with the assumption that Herodotus was an exponent of democracy (though one would expect a demo-

[20] F. D. Harvey, *Historia* 15 (1966), 255.
[21] See Jacoby, *RE Suppl.* II. 357. 46ff.

crat to make 'democracy' more specifically the object of praise). But it is also compatible with the assumption that he could admire a free government, whatever its more particular form. The quality of *eleutheria* fostered by any government seems to have been for Herodotus the ultimate touchstone of its worth. And in this respect it is clear that his admiration for the Spartan government was even more intense than any feeling he evinced for Athenian democracy. For Demaratus' characterization of the Spartans[22] in a closely comparable passage, where the context is freedom and the capacity and willingness to fight for it, concludes with a ringing endorsement of the Spartan system: 'For though they be free men, they are not in all respects free; Law is the master whom they own, and this master they fear more than your subjects fear you. Whatever it commands they do; and its commandment is always the same: it forbids them to flee in battle, whatever the number of their foes, and requires them to stand firm, and either to conquer or die.' Athenian *isegoria* is balanced, at least, by Spartan law: Herodotus, it would appear, was politically too moderate to be an idealogue. An Athenian democrat would have judged differently of Sparta; Herodotus was wise enough to perceive and applaud the merits of different governments as long as each contributed to *eleutheria*. In this passage about *isegoria* we see Herodotus' approval of the Athenian rejection of tyranny for democracy. The aspect of democracy which he praises is the internal freedom of the citizenry in contrast with tyrannic oppression. Probably that is why he used the word *isegoria*. It is the freedom implicit in democracy which is 'worth taking seriously', not the form of government giving power to the *demos* which here is praised. And while we may believe that he applauded the *isegoria* of Periclean democracy, that assumption does not suggest the further conclusion that his politics coincided with Pericles'.

Herodotus' most fundamental political convictions are

[22] Hdt. VII. 102–4 (cf. the *adynaton* of V. 92 α). The passage quoted is 104. 4. Demaratus is plainly speaking for Herodotus: see below, n. 25. (Rawlinson's translation.)

compatible with the claims and achievements of Athenian democracy, but they are consistent also with other Greek forms of government, the one exception being despotism, and his ultimate preference seems to have been aristocratic. As Jacoby has said,[23] 'Herodotus never entirely conquered his preference for Sparta.' Although the rhetorical emphasis of this statement implies that Herodotus' better nature strove to overcome a weakness, there is no reason to suspect any such internal struggle. The remark in V. 97. 2, where Herodotus observes that the many are more easily fooled than a single person, betrays his prejudice.[24] The numerous passages in which he simply accepts as natural and self-evident the pre-eminency of Spartan devotion to freedom is an even surer guide to his sympathies. Even the famous 'encomium' of the Athenians in VII. 139 rests on a significant presupposition. If the Athenians had medized the Spartans eventually would either have died fighting or finally have been forced to capitulate. It never occurred to him to reverse things: the Athenians were crucial but Sparta was a rock. An Englishman, a Churchill, could say of America's contribution to the Second World War precisely what Herodotus has said of Athens. Latent in Herodotus' judgement is the presupposition that Sparta's loyalty to the cause of liberty was absolute. 'Brave are all the Greeks who dwell in any Dorian land, but what I am about to say does not concern all, but only the Lacedaemonians. First then, come what may, they will never accept your terms, which would reduce Greece to slavery; and further, they are sure to join battle with you, though all the rest of the Greeks should submit to your will.'[25]

---

[23] *RE Suppl.* II. 357. 52f.

[24] Schmid-Stählin, *Griechiche Literaturgeschichte* I. 2. 621, are in the grip of their own conception of the democratic Herodotus when they claim that the Herodotean conception of happiness as illustrated by Tellus of Athens and Cleobis and Biton is the '*bürgerlich-demokratische*' view. The aristocratic terminology embedded in I. 30 offers a surer guide. The word *eunomia* in I. 65, as used of Sparta, furthermore, is not a mere label (cf. II. 124).

[25] Hdt. VII. 102. 2, Rawlinson's translation. As Macan said (ad loc.), Herodotus 'drops the mask.' His glorification of the Athenians in IX. 27 is

Herodotus' admiration of *isegoria*, although it can be taken as an endorsement of this aspect of the internal policies of the Periclean democracy, cannot suggest Herodotus' endorsement of the foreign policy of the Periclean state. Yet this is, or should be, part of what we mean when we speak of Periclean Athens. Certainly her foreign policy was her most visible and important characteristic to any non-Athenian. It is an instructive commentary on romantic attitudes that the many pages written about Herodotus' devotion to Pericles and his government, even of his having come first to appreciate in Athens the meaning of freedom because 'in the city of the Tyrannoktonoi such a view found its most powerful nourishment',[26] contain scarcely a reference to the imperial policy which chiefly defined that state *vis-à-vis* the others. Herodotus' sympathy for Athens, like his admiration for the government of the Spartans, derives from his devotion to freedom and his recognition that individual freedom may be secured by more than one means. But his estimate of the inherent worth of any state would of necessity transcend his theoretical judgement of its ideological merits. An *arche* imposing *douleia* would not have been popular with him.[27] He was wise enough, apparently, to be tolerant of Athens' course. But if there is any correlation between the spirited love of freedom implicit in his work and the sympathies he actually possessed, the Athenian government could not have incited either admiration or partisanship.

Yet it is almost a truism that Herodotus was the fervent

---

hardly comparable. In that passage, the Athenians are praising themselves. Demaratus' *persona* in VII. 102ff. is clearly that of the wise and 'objective' adviser. The view of Sparta here expressed is consistently maintained by Herodotus; it is the keystone of the Greek defence. See VII. 209, where Macan observed that the passage 'makes the attitude and action of Sparta the supreme and crucial question for the Persian king, and implicitly claims the credit of the Greek deliverance for Sparta.'

[26] Schmid-Stählin, op. cit., p. 578.

[27] G. E. M. De Ste. Croix, *Historia* 3 (1954–5), 1 ff., and those who follow him in reassessing the 'popularity' of the Athenian Empire would probably agree that Herodotus will have been of Thucydides' mind by class, instinct, persuasion, and sheer propriety of moral judgement.

admirer of Pericles.[28] We would, naturally, have it so. Jacoby, who was very cautious about Herodotus' attitude to democracy, perhaps because of it, in order to make intelligible his conception of Herodotus as the defender of Athens, postulated for Herodotus a strong attachment to Pericles. The picture he painted is not flattering to the author. 'The statesman clearly understood how to win over the widely travelled Halicarnassian whose knowledge of the world did not dispel a naïve confidence in assertions firmly made by people of authority, whose easily influenced mind merely sought what it could marvel at and love. That Pericles could learn much from him and perhaps stood to him as he did to Protagoras and Anaxagoras is not very likely. . . . Pericles did not learn from Herodotus but Herodotus from Pericles.'[29] It is not impossible, of course, that Pericles captivated Herodotus, though what is known about Pericles' personality, his austerity and his intellectual interests does not suggest that these men would have very much in common. Nor have Pericles' policies and statecraft, which compelled the admiration of a Thucydides, the qualities we might independently suppose Herodotus would be apt to find congenial. Certainly they elicited no detectable appreciation in the *Histories*. But that Herodotus was the simpleton Jacoby here suggests is simply unbelievable. Indeed, the statement I have quoted is of value primarily because it shows how much Jacoby had to stretch things in order to motivate Herodotus' alleged enthusiasm. There is too little common ground between these men to justify the association by an appeal to sympathies shared. Herodotus, to be the admirer of Pericles, needed to be swept away—a little boy sitting at the feet of the Olympian. Again it is a case of extrapolating Herodotus' opinion from Thucydides' convictions without regard for the fact that Thucydides' opinions derive from a different moral and intellectual standpoint.

---

[28] Strasburger, loc. cit., combated this view.
[29] *RE Suppl.* II. 240. 61ff.

It is an odd enthusiasm which led Herodotus to conceal his own opinion and resolutely to avoid mention of Pericles except in one remarkable passage. Whether this passage has fostered the traditional view of Herodotus' adulation of Pericles or whether that preconception has informed the usual interpretation of the passage would be difficult to say. But, as in the other cases, it is again a question of inference. With solemn words, after setting forth the lineage of the Alcmeonids in a context that begins by defending them from the charge of medism (VI. 121–4), testifies to the great importance of that family (125) and passes on to the wedding of Agariste (126–30), Herodotus concludes by stating that Agariste the daughter of Cleisthenes, married to Xanthippus the son of Ariphron, had a dream in her sleep when she was pregnant, and she dreamed she gave birth to a lion. 'A few days later Pericles was born.'

Although most discussions of the symbol turn on the 'meaning' of 'lion' it is unlikely that such meaning was automatically and inevitably fixed by any symbolic code, any more than the 'stream of water' of I. 107, the vine of I. 108, or any other hint from the supernatural. But how this *teras* could have been suggestive of good or implicit of praise I cannot see.[30] It is surely wrong to assume that the lion was a mere simile and to modify the symbol by supposing, anachronistically, that Herodotus meant that Pericles would turn out to be as courageous as Richard the Lion-heart. The lion was not a friendly beast; it was a wild and man-eating animal, in Homer, the symbol of bone-crushing force. And even if we would like our sons to be 'lions' it is because they are terrible to others and not to us.[31] To me, therefore, there is something ominous and terrible in the dream precisely because it concerns a man whose power was great. It does not 'mean' that Pericles was predictively a monster but it suggests, as

---

[30] H. Nissen, *Historische Zeitschrift* 63 (1889), 420, Focke, *Herodot als Historiker*, pp. 29ff., Strasburger, loc. cit., p. 29, pointed out that the symbol is ambivalent.

[31] Aristophanes, *Thesm.* 514.

inevitably as the vine and the water, that he was something
more and less than human, something to be feared, a terrific
phenomenon in the strict sense of the word. And Herodotus,
by avoiding any explanation of the *teras*, by providing no
interpretation, has left it up to his hearers to determine what
the meaning may be. That the audience he was addressing
felt differently about Pericles than do we, that they were
afraid of Athenian power, that their predominant emotion
will not have been admiration, is the important guide.[32]
From their perspective the omen could not have been a
source of comfort and Herodotus gave no explanation or
qualification to change that perspective.

Herodotus amply testified to the greatness of the
Alcmeonid clan from which Pericles was sprung on his
mother's side. The inference that Pericles' influence upon him
provides the explanation is unnecessary. The importance of
that clan for the history of Athens is indisputable.[33] Only
clear signs that he overrated it systematically would suggest
partiality on his part to Pericles. Are there such signs? His
appraisal seems objective. Yet Jacoby has listed four passages
illustrating Herodotus' partiality to the clan: V. 69, 78;
VIII. 17; IX. 114. Let us consider them.

The description of Cleisthenes' reforms in V. 69 is cast in
the neutral and unemotional terms of an elementary struggle

---

[32] It is worth adding, in support of this consideration, that although G. W.
Dyson, *Classical Quarterly* 23 (1929), 187f., could conclude from his study of the
oracle quoted in V. 92 that 'no conclusion whatever can be drawn' from the
lion mentioned there, the Labdacids missed the ambiguity and tried to murder
Cypselus.

[33] His use of this clan as a source of information was a natural step permitting
no inference about his personal attitudes. He also borrowed from Philaid
tradition (VI. 34ff., 103ff.), and no Alcmeonid is treated as splendidly as
Miltiades at Marathon, not to mention the same treatment of that figure, which
is quite gratuitous, in IV. 137f. Jacoby's belief (*RE Suppl.* II. 413. 53ff.) that
Herodotus fell 'more strongly' under the spell of the Alcmeonids is a consequence of his opinion that Herodotus was an admirer of Pericles. The passages
he adduces to prove it will be considered above. Whether Herodotus' defence of
the Alcmeonids from the charge of treason in 490 B.C. (VI. 121–4) is the mark of
a special tie or a fair-minded attitude can be determined only by what can be
inferred from his treatment of the clan elsewhere.

for power. Here, if anywhere, was the place for an encomium
of Cleisthenes or of the democracy. But neither in this chapter, nor in the next, where Herodotus states that the Alcmeonids were held responsible for a sacrilegious murder, is
there any obvious laudation.[34] However, there is one notable
point about his description of Cleisthenes' actions which,
perhaps because it seems foolish to us, tends to be discounted.
It is contained in V. 67, where Herodotus provides us with
what he considers to have been the motive of Cleisthenes in
instituting his tribal reform. 'In this, it seems to me, this
Cleisthenes imitated his maternal grandfather Cleisthenes
the tyrant of Sicyon.' Whether Herodotus is right or wrong
matters not at all. What is significant is that he is irreverent
as to Cleisthenes' motive and, by implication, cynical about
the entire proceeding.

V. 78, the passage on *isegoria*, we have already considered.
It does not imply an Alcmeonid source or even promote an
Alcmeonid claim. Is it an accident that in V. 78, where
isegoria is praised, we hear nothing of the Alcmeonids, and
in V. 69, where Cleisthenes' reforms are mentioned, there is
an absence of praise? There is, of course, nothing extraordinary about this *unless* it be presumed that he was a proponent of the Alcmeonids.

Herodotus' inclusion of the *aristeia* of Cleinias son of
Alcibiades in VIII. 17, is at best a marginal propagandistic
feat. Not enough is made of it by Herodotus to suggest that
it is a compliment.

Finally, IX. 114. Xanthippus son of Ariphron, Pericles'
father, is denoted in 114 as the commander of the Athenian
contingent which, after the battle of Mycale, separated from
the Spartans and proceeded to the investment of Sestus.
Since it is Herodotus' invariable habit to supply the names of
the leaders of any force (is VII. 107 a compliment to the

---

[34] Pohlenz, *Herodot*, p. 167, understands V. 71 as high praise for the Alcmeonids: they slew a would-be tyrant. Jacoby, *Atthis* (Oxford, 1949), p. 187, thinks
the story exculpatory. *We* may excuse or even praise them for their act. But it is
erroneous to project such inferences into an account that does not imply them
and which instead centres on the sacrilege.

Philaids?) his naming of Xanthippus is perfectly neutral. The claim, moreover, that the energetic and conscientious action of the Athenians to which allusion is made in 117 is a tribute to Xanthippus[35] requires that we interpolate into Herodotus' indefinite phrase 'the generals' the name Xanthippus. The process may be easy enough. But the need for it suggests that Herodotus was not concerned to single him out for praise. Rather has he hid his light under a bushel. Finally, it is impossible to see how in 120. 4 there is an intentional reference to Xanthippus' incorruptibility 'which probably is intended to contrast with Themistocles' behaviour.'[36] Here, Xanthippus the general refuses to accept money offered to the Athenians in return for the life of Artayctes and his son. His lofty motive? 'For the Elaiousians, desiring to avenge Protesilaus, wanted him to be done away with, and the general himself concurred.' If Herodotus had intended the compliments some have assumed, his task was accomplished very badly. But he missed a comparable opportunity when treating of Xanthippus at Mycale. As Macan justly observed at IX. 114, 'not much credit is given him for the victory at Mykale.'

Herodotus' treatment of the Alcmeonids is not admiring but objective. It indicates the importance of this family but not his captivation by it. Because he was fair minded we make him into a partisan.[37] It is the same with his treatment of Athens. One effect of Herodotus' history of the Persian Wars is that Athens' achievements are appreciated justly. But no evidence other than that fact suggests that he was incited to choose this subject in order to justify the contemporary

---

[35] Jacoby, *RE Suppl.* II. 467. 48ff.

[36] Ibid.

[37] Herodotus, clearly, scatters praise and blame without any evident direction. An author predisposed to the Alcmeonids would not have ignored the opportunities his own account provided to contribute to their reputation. As a pendant to the defence of the Alcmeonids in VI. 121–4 we need only consider his description of Megacles in I. 59–64. No pro-Alcmeonid would have described Megacles in this fashion. Were it not for Herodotus, in fact, the record of the Alcmeonids would be cleaner.

policies of the Athenian state or otherwise to fulfil an apologetic purpose. It is unreasonable to suppose that Herodotus would so effectively and resolutely have concealed the intention that is supposed to have animated him. It is psychologically implausible that anyone so animated could have proceeded in his level-headed fashion. There is something that smells of the lamp in the conception that Herodotus wrote about the victory of the Greeks over the barbarians as he has done in order to make the point ever so subtly that the Athenians were unjustly maligned. The idea that he believed his contemporaries would look more kindly upon the Athenians and their empire because once they had distinguished themselves above all others in defending Greek freedom deprives Herodotus of the most elementary awareness of human nature and psychology. He knew his contemporaries, as he showed in VII. 139. They would have said, as Sthenelaidas said (Thuc. I. 86. 1), 'I do not understand this multitude of words of the Athenians. They praise themselves greatly but do not deny that they are injuring our allies and the Peloponnesus. And yet if they once were true against the Mede but unjust now to us they deserve a double penalty because in the place of good men they have become bad.'

Herodotus' motive in writing his history was not a narrow one. He did not attempt to justify the Athenian Empire and Periclean Athens nor does his work accomplish that objective. Such a motive would be incompatible with the breadth and depth of his sympathies. Had he been actuated in the manner alleged, he could not have treated the Spartans as he has done, nor would the pan-Hellenic sentiment which is one of the traits of his history have been so keenly evoked. His position is more ambiguous; it is harder to label than that of a partisan. Though he was not a proponent of Periclean imperialism he was not guided by hatred of that city. It is precisely this which makes it difficult to judge his position. For in that period of antitheses, with Athens opposed to Sparta and democracy to oligarchy, Herodotus somehow managed to be involved, as the *Histories* attest, and yet objective. He is too detached to be an Athenian propagandist and too complex to permit his intent to be extracted by inference from an isolated passage. If that is recognized, a considerable obstacle in the way of appreciating his method will be removed.

IV

HERODOTUS' PERSPECTIVE

THUCYDIDES believed and claimed that he had written a κτῆμα ἐς αἰεί—a possession for all time (I. 22. 4). The boast may have struck his contemporaries as arrogant and rhetorical. To the modern world it is a truism. Our consciousness of the perfect justification of these words, however, deprives them of impact and robs them of all but superficial meaning. Yet their value is inestimable. They tell us, if we needed to be told, what stance he had adopted, what perspective he had taken, in writing his history. These words explain the principle of his selection and inclusion of material. Thinking of future generations more than of his immediate audience, his task as he defined it was to create a history of the Peloponnesian War that would be self-explanatory; no special knowledge beyond his own history would be required to secure perfect comprehension of the important and universally relevant issues. He neither played upon the knowledge of his contemporaries nor allowed that knowledge to deflect him from his course. He would not be constrained to include matter which his audience might well expect to find—gossip about Pericles, intra-political strife, etc.[1] Thus he divorced his account as much as he could from what he considered intrinsically irrelevant, whatever the expectations of his audience may have been, and he included material which they hardly needed to be told in order to make the picture clear to future generations lacking the specific knowledge of contemporaries.[2] Thucydides' sense of the

[1] Gomme's summary of 'what Thucydides takes for granted' (*Commentary* I. 1–25) illustrates how little Thucydides ignored what was strictly relevant to his subject, however important these omissions for our comprehension of the period.

[2] See, e.g., Thuc. II. 48. 3, the plague, and VIII. 2, his description of the

future is one of the most remarkable aspects of his genius. It
dominates his history and justifies his boast. For this reason he
is to us not only the most brilliant of historians but also, from
our point of view, one of the most satisfactory. Although we
miss a good deal by not seeing the world he described through
the eyes of his contemporaries, and although we may question whether in certain cases he may not have omitted data
important for our comprehension of the war, nevertheless,
his conception of history or, rather, of the audience for which
he was writing, guarantees that his history of the Peloponnesian War leaves nothing he considered relevant taken for
granted.

The same sentence in which Thucydides proclaims the
eternal relevance of his work ends by contrasting it with a
'declamation intended for a momentary display'—ἀγώνισμα
ἐς τὸ παραχρῆμα ἀκούειν. The reference is to Herodotus; only
his predecessor can here be intended. Thucydides is alluding
to an historical work literally comparable to his own, one
which was written, as ἀγώνισμα suggests, in a highly wrought
and artistic fashion. That is enough to exclude the more
austere and even scholarly works of Herodotus' predecessors
and such later contemporaries as Hellanicus of Lesbos. The
disapprobation contained in Thucydides' remark is hardly
malicious or spiteful. Rather is it a consequence of what, in
Thucydides' view, history should be and what Herodotus
failed to make it. It reflects Thucydides' belief that Herodotus' perspective was wrong, that his great work was
directed to a particular audience at a particular moment in
time. In a word, Thucydides wrote for the future, Herodotus
for his contemporaries. And in doing so, Herodotus, as
Thucydides was very much aware, was incomplete and misleading or would eventually become so through the passage
of time. That is probably one of the reasons Thucydides was
moved to supplement his predecessor in several important

---

state of mind in Hellas. But it is enough to say that Thucydides was writing
contemporary history.

details, as we shall see. It is enough to say here, however, that their difference in perspective, in their conception of the audience to which they were speaking, is of the greatest importance in attaining a just estimation of Herodotus' intent and method. For judged by our accustomed standards, Herodotus' technique is distinctly unusual. We have misconstrued him because automatically we read him in the same way that we read other historians such as Thucydides, who set the standard for all who follow. Although Thucydides wrote a work with an eye to later generations and attempted to present his material as scientifically as possible, Herodotus directed himself exclusively to his own generation. Only by reading him as if we were his contemporaries can his intentions be fully understood.

One further contrast between Herodotus and Thucydides, which is the corollary of that already mentioned, relates to the manner in which each of them present their material. If Thucydides is eminently 'scientific', Herodotus is essentially an artist. Herodotus' work, especially the last three books, is neither narrative nor 'drama', but something of both. He owed much to the *Iliad* and the *Odyssey*, as frequently has been pointed out. In spirit, however, and in general effect, his work is most like to the Athenian drama.[3] Herodotus' reticence, his reliance on understatement, is the reticence of the dramatist who expresses his opinion through the characters of his creation. Though Herodotus could comment in his own person about whatever he wished, and does so frequently enough, this 'Ionic' and pedagogical strain in his work recedes in proportion as his work becomes dramatic. In VII–IX, for instance, he separates himself carefully from those scenes of greatest dramatic impact. Precisely as the audiences of Aeschylus and Sophocles were intended to form their conclusions without the explicit aid of the playwright, so does Herodotus demand or expect an involved audience participating in and judging what is evoked before them. Herodotus' artistic method is to lead the hearer by what he

[3] See Schmid-Stählin, *Griechische Literaturgeschichte* I. 2. 569f.

does not say as much as by what he does. Irony, pathos, paradox, and tragedy develop from his tacit dialogue with his audience. But it is a contemporary audience, whose expectations he could predict, not some future generation with different expectations, for which he was writing.

The truth of these contentions should become apparent from the examination of two test cases. His treatment of Pausanias and Themistocles has frequently been considered problematical or at least surprising. Both are excellent examples of his method and his standpoint.

Herodotus portrays Pausanias, the Regent of Sparta, as if he were the epitome of the knight *sans peur et sans reproche*. The picture he paints is one of the most detailed in the *Histories*—a companion piece to that of Themistocles. Unquestionably he expended the greatest care and thought in the elaboration of the picture, which is consistent and obtrusive. He tells us emphatically that at Plataea Pausanias 'won the finest victory of any man of whom we know' (IX. 64), and Pausanias is told substantially the same thing by a noble Aeginetan, Lampon son of Pytheus. 'O son of Cleombrotus, you have accomplished a great and splendid feat. God has granted you, since you have saved Greece, to lay up in store the greatest glory of any Greek of whom we know' (IX. 78). Shortly thereafter, Pausanias, whose attempt to keep the spoil secure is noted (IX. 80. 1), is granted a tenth of it (IX. 81. 2). Herodotus then relates that extraordinary story which has Pausanias look upon Xerxes' oriental luxury, that equipage which he gave over to Mardonius when he fled from Greece. Pausanias orders the servants to prepare the kind of dinner they were accustomed to serve to Mardonius (IX. 82. 2). 'They did as they were bid and then Pausanias, after he saw the richly covered couches of gold and silver, and the gold and silver tables, and the dazzling display of the dinner, was thunderstruck by the good things set before him. He ordered his own servants to prepare a Laconian feast for the humour of it. After the dinner was prepared Pausanias laughed since the difference was great. He summoned the Greek generals and when they came Pausanias said, pointing to the display of each of the dinners, "I have assembled you because I want to show you the folly of the Mede. With a way of life such as this he came to take away from us our miserable fare." This it is said that Pausanias remarked to the generals.' In IX. 88, Pausanias shows compassion and charity to the children of men guilty of treachery. One further anecdote concerns Pausanias' solicitous and lofty treatment of a misused woman (IX. 76).

Herodotus' description of the Regent is surprising on two counts. In the first place, the dramatic acknowledgement of his personal contribution is unusual and surprisingly emphatic. Herodotus' interest is frankly biographical: the man interests him as much as his achievement. His account is also surprising in view of Pausanias' subsequent career and lamentable end. The question of his intent in depicting Pausanias as he has done, in sparing no effort to portray him as an extraordinarily noble and fortunate figure, naturally suggests itself. The question cannot be skirted by invoking a source hypothetically concerned to magnify Pausanias' role in 479 B.C.[4] That the recollection of Pausanias' greatness managed to survive the obloquy cast upon his name is not to be believed—he was not another Nero, with people setting flowers on his grave. In any event, Herodotus' presentation must be the mirror of his own attitude and that presentation reveals a uniform conception of the Spartan Regent. For this reason, some have concluded that Herodotus' account of Pausanias is governed by scepticism about his guilt, that a natural implication of Herodotus' sketch is that he did not consider Pausanias to be the scoundrel others supposed.[5]

Nothing could be farther from the truth. What surprises us is precisely what Herodotus was counting on but what we do

---

[4] We cannot postulate a favourable Delphic source from Thuc. I. 134. 4, since the sacrilegious action of the Spartans in murdering Pausanias explains the Delphic injunction to provide twin statues of him.

[5] See H. Strasburger, *Historia* 4 (1955), 34.

The man interests him as much as his achievements.

not expect because this is a 'historical work'. It is almost as if we assume that Herodotus intended to write a competing version. When 'historians' are good to villainous characters they are setting the record straight, combating an erroneous tradition, repeating an apologetic source. We are so accustomed to completing Herodotus' account of Pausanias by adding to it as a matter of course the final chapters as recorded by Thucydides that we have forgotten that Herodotus could not know that Thucydides would tell of Pausanias' end. When we realize that he thought in no such terms, that he was confronting his audience independently and alone, the conclusion is as revealing as it is startling. If *we* had only Herodotus on the subject of Pausanias, the son of Cleombrotus would indeed 'have laid up the greatest store of glory of any Greek'. It certainly did not occur to Herodotus that he could mislead anyone in this fashion. There is not the slightest reason to suppose that he could have wished to. It follows inescapably that Herodotus took for granted the knowledge of Pausanias' fall. Herodotus' intention was to build upon that knowledge; the reflections of his contemporaries are the precondition of his narrative. They believed, and Herodotus knew they believed, that Pausanias was a traitor. Herodotus' dramatic treatment of Pausanias takes its departure and acquires its significance from the common knowledge of his time. His portrait of Pausanias is in the light of that knowledge a masterpiece of irony and a harbinger of tragedy. Lampon's words have a double meaning. 'God has granted you to lay up in store the greatest glory of any Greek.' What God granted Pausanias threw away. The implicit lesson is not the less immediate because Herodotus studiously avoided any allusion to Pausanias' later *hybris*.[6] On the contrary, it is the more impressive because of it. Herodotus has characterized the finest hour of a man whose degeneration provides a striking example of Herodotus' law of history, of the in-

---

[6] Hdt. VIII. 3. 2 is too removed in context to affect matters. Note, though, that the manner of his allusion to Pausanias' '*hybris*' indicates that it was common knowledge.

stability of good fortune: σκοπέειν δὲ χρὴ παντὸς χρήματος τὴν τελευτὴν κῇ ἀποβήσεται (I. 32. 9). That is why his treatment of Pausanias is so carefully done and so eminent a feature of the ninth book.

Herodotus' method is artistic, not historical. He has created a drama to which the audience, as the 'dramatist' well knows, and indeed demands, will bring a level of comprehension that altogether changes its point. What appear to be mere anecdotes without direction are in reality magnificent and richly allusive passages. From the point of view of the audience, that fascination of Pausanias with the luxury of the Persians will have been only too clear. The vision proved too much for him. Herodotus, in depicting the scene, foreshadowed that later disaster and presupposed the knowledge of it. As a final example of his method, one so rich in irony that it needs no comment, let us consider the brave speech Pausanias delivers in refusing to maltreat the corpse of Mardonius, as was suggested by the same Lampon (IX. 79). 'O friend from Aegina, I am delighted by your good feeling and solicitude. Nevertheless you have strayed from sound judgement. For having raised me high in respect to fatherland and deed, you bring me down to nothing by urging me to do injury to the dead, saying that if I do this my fame will be greater. This is a thing a barbarian may suitably do and not a Greek. And them we despise. In this matter, therefore, I would neither desire to please the Aeginetans nor anyone else who desires it. It is enough for me to please the Spartans by acting piously and by speaking piously. And I say that Leonidas, whom you urge me to honour, has been honoured greatly. He and the rest of the dead at Thermopylae are honoured by the numberless wraiths of these men here. Do not you then approach me or advise me if you remain in the same opinion but be thankful that you go off unharmed.'

It is a magnificently ironic and tragic picture. One thinks of Oedipus damning himself, condemning what will prove to be his own tragic flaw. But this picture could be misleading; it depends on knowledge that is taken for granted. Perhaps that explains Thucydides' supplementary account. He may have felt obliged to provide it in order to keep the historical record unambiguous and free from what easily could become a deceptive tradition. Thucydides certainly was capable of such prognosis. It is also, I think, a superb example of what Thucydides had in mind when he spoke of the 'prize composition for the moment'. For Herodotus' concern was with the minds and emotions of his listeners, not with the inferences of later generations or the requirements of 'scientific' history. His account of Pausanias was an imaginative recreation calculated to achieve maximum psychological effect. His contemporaries unquestionably responded as he expected.

No person is depicted by Herodotus with more care and more skill than Themistocles. It is therefore illustrative of the manner in which Herodotus has been studied, of the presuppositions which we bring to our reading of his work, that his portrait of Themistocles has been held up as an example of Herodotus' malignity and incomprehension. Ivo Bruns, in his excellent study of biography, helped to formulate this prevalent view.[7] In speaking of Herodotus' Themistocles he claimed that Herodotus, unlike Thucydides, lacked a clear conception 'of the nature of his characters and stood helplessly before the most contradictory traditions'. That opinion is misconceived. Far from lacking a conception of Themistocles' personality, Herodotus is responsible for having created it. He presents us with a person whose distinguishing characteristics are cleverness and foresight on the one hand and greed and unscrupulousness on the other. The problem has not been that Herodotus lacks a self-consistent idea of Themistocles but that we evidently would prefer a different conception. And that preference has facilitated the view that Herodotus was either unaccountably malicious or that he mechanically reproduced 'hostile traditions' without clearly knowing what he was doing. It is ironic that an author who is

[7] *Das literarische Porträt der Griechen* (Berlin, 1896), p. 89.

supposed to have written an encomium of Athens is suspected of malignancy towards that state's greatest hero and is regarded as incapable of distinguishing a 'hostile' tradition from a favourable one.

Herodotus' 'intent' deserves clearer analysis than it has received. When, for example, Themistocles is described essentially as the sort of man 'openly filling his pockets at every opportunity',[8] is Herodotus malignant or uncomprehending because Themistocles was actually known to have been honest? The charge of cupidity levelled against him is an ancient one.[9] Was Herodotus hostile, then, because it is a mark of hostility not to have suppressed this objectionable trait? Herodotus assuredly did not write his history in order to present Themistocles as if he were the hero of a nineteenth-century novel. The important consideration for judging Herodotus' historical perception is that he recognized Themistocles' genius and resource and, more important, that the picture he paints of Themistocles is one which permits *us* to recognize his greatness. For Themistocles is the dominant figure in his account of Xerxes' War.

Again, I suggest, the cardinal assumption has been that Herodotus was writing 'scientific' history—that he intended his sketch of Themistocles to be a straight-forward 'historical' portrayal like that of Thucydides.[10] Thucydides, from his perspective, wanted future generations to realize that the intelligence and the foresight of Themistocles were crucial factors in the development of the Athenian state. His moral character and even the question of whether he became treasonable are irrelevant to that concern—not, by any means, that his own opinion of Themistocles' character is noticeably different from Herodotus'. Thucydides' emphasis is different. Herodotus, though he provides us with the material permitting us to form a proper estimate of Themistocles' intellectual capacity, was concerned to present a dramatic portrait of this figure which would be credible to

---

[8] Meyer, *Forschungen* II. 223.   [9] Timocreon, Frag. 1, Diehl.
[10] Thuc. I. 135ff.

his contemporaries. He was dealing with the expectations of his audience. Merely consider, for instance, that oft-discussed and unappreciated first mention of Themistocles made by Herodotus in VII. 143. 'Now there was a certain Athenian man who recently had stepped up to the forefront whose name was Themistocles and who was called the son of Neocles'—ἦν δὲ τῶν τις Ἀθηναίων ἀνὴρ ἐς πρώτους νεωστὶ παριών, τῷ οὔνομα μὲν ἦν Θεμιστοκλέης, παῖς δὲ Νεοκλέος ἐκαλέετο.

Most commentators consider this introduction a slap.[11] Would his audience have thought so on hearing it? Herodotus has just finished describing very dramatically the plight of Athens, the fact that 'authority' was against any attempt to fight a sea-battle at Salamis (which the audience well knew was crucial). Dark was the moment; 'but there was a certain Athenian man who had recently stepped to the fore-front'. The first two words, ἦν δέ, are enough to show a rift in the clouds. And then, deliberately, the name is withheld until the sentence runs to its end. Expectation, suspense and understatement: Herodotus has given Themistocles a drum-roll. The formula is an excellent one with which to start an important episode. Homer used it to introduce Dolon (*Iliad* X. 314). The tone of such an introduction is nicely indicated by Xenophon in *Anabasis* III. 1. 4. At a critical moment, when the Greek mercenaries faced crisis, Xenophon introduced the hero with these words: 'Now there was a certain man in the army, Xenophon the Athenian'—ἦν δέ τις ἐν τῇ στρατιᾷ Ξενοφῶν Ἀθηναῖος. We seem to expect that Herodotus should have provided us with some reference to Themistocles' earlier career (assuming he had knowledge of it) or have made some weighty historical judgement when actually his own concern was dramatic.[12]

---

[11] Macan is the exception.

[12] The claim that Herodotus should have referred in this context to the earlier archonship of Themistocles (assuming that it is historical—which does not follow from Thuc. I. 93. 3) examples the modern demand that Herodotus provide us with 'historical fact' without particular relevance to his own account.

Let us therefore consider Herodotus' Themistocles from the point of view of his audience. The artistic and dramatic problems which the expectations of his audience would have created for him, if his account was to be successful, were considerable. Whatever his contemporaries may have known of Themistocles' contributions in 480–79 B.C. and however they viewed his epochal work in making Athens a sea-power, we may assume that he was chiefly pre-eminent as the personification of wiliness. The popular conception of this great man undoubtedly centred on his suppleness and craft. He had been condemned to death for treason and after a sensational flight to Persia had gained an extraordinary reception from the Great King. Themistocles' life was the kind to make people marvel; the final chapter of it would have been as notable and even more inciteful of speculation about the man and anecdotes about his nature than the earlier ones. His greatness may have been proved by his leadership in 480–79 B.C.; but to a later generation removed from that era the amazing dexterity and capacity to look after himself signalled by his final Asiatic venture will have been the most remarkable and most notorious of all. That final chapter must, for Herodotus, have been the starting point in his attempt to fathom the character of that remarkable man. The challenge to his skill was to create a believable character who was capable of being at once the saviour of the Greeks in Xerxes' War and the presumed traitor of not very long after. Herodotus married the known unscrupulous but invariably successful figure who died in Persia with the man who in 479 B.C. was proclaimed 'the wisest man in Greece' (VIII, 124. 1).

As in the case of Pausanias, Herodotus expected his audience to superimpose its knowledge of the sensational downfall of Themistocles on to his description of that character. Where we are apt to make him an abstraction, Herodotus gave him verisimilitude. An admirable instance of his technique is provided by his narration in VIII. 108ff. of Themistocles' famous message to Xerxes after the battle of

Salamis. The Greeks, having reached Andros in pursuit of
Xerxes, halted for a council of war (VIII. 108). Themistocles
as usual hit upon the most effective means to wound the
enemy and advanced the proposal that the Greeks race to the
Hellespont and dismantle the bridges.[13] We are reminded of
former occasions when the others are hostile to his bold and
successful measures. However, though Herodotus could
attribute the resolve to Themistocles, the nature of the case
forbade him from presenting us here with the successful
operation of his powers or his craft. The plan was not
attempted. Yet Themistocles' defeat is but temporary, for he
is able to capitalize even on that. 'When he understood that
he would not persuade the many, at any rate, he changed
course with the Athenians. For they were especially grieved
at the thought of the Persians escaping, and were eager to sail
to the Hellespont even if the others did not want to and even
if they must act alone.' Themistocles then dissuades them
with an effective speech and Herodotus resumes (VIII. 109.
5): 'This he said intending to lay up store with the Persian in
order that he might have some place of refuge if by some ·
chance a disaster should come upon him from the Athenians.
And this was the very thing that happened. Themistocles de-
ceived them in his speech and the Athenians were persuaded'
to give up the venture. Sicinnus was thereupon sent by
Themistocles to tell Xerxes that 'Themistocles, desiring to do
Xerxes a service, *stopped the Greeks* when they wished to pursue his ships and break down the bridges at the Hellespont'
(VIII. 110. 3).

Eduard Meyer excoriated Herodotus for this story. He
believed that Herodotus intended to make Themistocles
responsible for 'the betrayal of the Greek cause'.[14] Macan
and Stein assume the phrase 'intending to lay up store of
credit with Xerxes' 'shows how much prejudiced Herodotus
is ... even in a case where not a shadow of suspicion falls on

---

[13] Herodotus has prepared us to recognize the importance of such an action.
It is what Xerxes feared—VIII. 97. Cf. VII. 10. 2; VIII. 102.
[14] *Forschungen* II. 223.

him.'[15] How, in his note to VIII. 110, writes that Herodotus is 'evidently here under the influence of traditions hostile to Themistocles. There is no special reason to suspect him of double dealing in this case.' Surely these scholars have studied the passage with the wrong lens. Herodotus' intent was to show Themistocles' great capacity for the clever ruse. Deceit, to be sure, is part of the nature Herodotus, like Thucydides,[16] supposed him to possess. That, after all, was the key to his strategic genius. But the purpose of the anecdote is not to show some treasonable intent on Themistocles' part. Herodotus went to considerable length to make that clear; one half of the episode should not be separated from the other. Themistocles was forestalled by his colleagues from inflicting the crushing blow that he had himself conceived of. If Herodotus had intended to make Themistocles a *traitor*, he would have presented the story differently. Themistocles did not deceive the Greeks;[17] he fooled Xerxes. His allegation that he had stopped the Greeks from racing to the Hellespont was the reverse of the truth. But Xerxes did not know it and so Themistocles laid up store of credit with the King.

What is worthy of especial note in Herodotus' narrative is the care he has taken *not* to suggest that Themistocles was already marching down the path of treason. Herodotus has attributed to Themistocles a remarkable instance of his famous foresight. But he put Themistocles' prevision in the most general terms—'If possibly (ἄρα) some evil fall upon him from the Athenians.'[18] His Themistocles viewed the

---

[15] Macan, ad loc.

[16] See the bribe and threat in I. 137. 2. In 137. 4 we have a reference to the message described by Herodotus. From that account it was clear that Themistocles was lying, as Thucydides says. Thucydides' abstract formulation of Themistocles genius in I. 138. 3, so often quoted as if in refutation of Herodotus, reads as if it were a judgement derived from Herodotus' own account, so little are the two incompatible.

[17] His deception of the Athenians was his concealment from them of his further intentions. Obviously they had to be dissuaded.

[18] The particle is important. See IX. 15. 2 for its lack.

6+H.

possibility of a dangerous turn in his career very hypothetically. Herodotus has separated the actual treason everyone thinks of from Themistocles' own prognostication. It is
a splendid example of Herodotus having it both ways, and
intentionally so.

What we, in an overprotective way, have taken to be an
anecdote derogatory of Themistocles would to his audience
have appeared to be the ultimate example of Themistocles'
capacity to look after himself. Herodotus did not intend to
suggest that Themistocles was a traitor to the Greek cause.
But he very definitely permitted that conception of Themistocles to illuminate his account. His purpose is artistic.[19] He
was attempting neither to blacken Themistocles' reputation
nor to whitewash it. He was recreating Themistocles' character for the sake of his story, not for the 'historical record'. If
we do not like this fifth-century Odysseus, it is perhaps because we are apt to glorify our heroes in more conventional
terms and because we are unaccustomed to finding this kind
of dramatization in a history. That was not the opinion of
Cicero[20] or, one suspects, of Thucydides. The Greeks were
not so prim in their younger days.[21] They could admire
cleverness and dexterity for their own sake. We have only to
think of Themistocles' predecessor and his protector's
attitude to *him*:

> Athena began to smile;
> She caressed him, her form now that of a woman,
> Beautiful, tall, skilled at weaving fine things.
> She spoke to him in winged words:

[19] So, for example, his mention of Mnesiphilus in VIII. 57f. is calculated to
give dramatic emphasis to the crucial moment at Salamis, not to deprive
Themistocles of credit. We are over-solicitous of Themistocles.

[20] *Ad fam.* V. 12. 7: *Atque hoc praestantius mihi fuerit et ad laetitiam animi et ad
memoriae dignitatem, si in tua scripta pervenere quam si in ceterorum, quod non ingenium
mihi solum suppeditatum fuerit tecum, sicut Timoleonti a Timaeo aut ab Herodote
Themistocli. . . .*

[21] By Plutarch's time, veneration for the heroes of the Persian War had become a matter of principle.

'Cunning and thievish the man who could beat you
In all your tricks, even if some god were to try it.
You devil! You schemer! Fraud! You never cease,
Not even at home, from the cheats
And lying words that are your nature.
But we'll say no more: we're both
Alike.'[22]

Herodotus' treatment of Themistocles, like that of
Pausanias, is directed to contemporaries well aware of what
he leaves unsaid. The impact derives from his reliance on
the response of his audience, from what he knows his hearers
will conclude. His procedure is not substantially different
from that of the tragedians. The basics were known, the end
result predictable. What mattered was the presentation of
the detail in such a way as to keep the audience involved and
make the pattern explicable. This is the essence of Herodotus'
art and the key to his technique. The instances already discussed provide what are perhaps the most remarkable
examples of this technique because of Herodotus' subtlety
and because his imaginative recreation was so daring. But
it is the same with Xerxes. No Greek was unaware that this
splendid figure would fall heavily and Herodotus, in presenting Xerxes to his audience, made him the more splendid
so that the fall would be more dramatic. In this case, to be
sure, our own presuppositions coincide with those of Herodotus' contemporaries. What I have tried to suggest,
however, is that this is not inevitably so, as the usual interpretation of his treatment of Pausanias and Themistocles
should show. When our expectations do not jibe with contemporary expectations, it is easy to misconstrue Herodotus'
intentions as being to 'exculpate' Pausanias or to 'vilify'
Themistocles. We expect him to 'tell the truth' where he
expected his contemporaries to use 'the truth' as the touchstone of his account. How different might our interpretation
of Herodotus' portraits of Pausanias and Themistocles have
been if we realized that in both cases Herodotus expected

[22] *Odyssey* XIII. 287–97.

his audience to be thinking primarily of the fall of each man. Instead we have assumed that these final stages of each man's career were unimportant for Herodotus or, rather, that Pausanias' was unimportant. For in the instance of Themistocles, it is we who dissociate that final chapter from the earlier and virtually condemn Herodotus for remembering it. The difference between Herodotus and Thucydides, between the *Histories* and 'history', is at once subtle and profound.

We must therefore think away the predisposition to approach Herodotus as if he were speaking to us directly, and understand him, as best we can, as his contemporaries would have done. There are fundamental but unspoken connections he relied on his audience to make. In this respect, also, we must abandon that general willingness to judge events from a perspective favourable to Athens, to assume that everyone shared it. The projection of that attitude into Herodotus has made his sympathies seem a chaos of inconsistency. Herodotus did not write his history for the partisans of the Athenian democracy. He directed his work to the Greek world in general and more particularly to a class which he, like Thucydides (II. 8. 4) considered hostile to the state of Athens.[23] Finally, since it is Herodotus' technique to mesh his narrative with the predictable thoughts of his contemporaries, we must remind ourselves constantly that the people for whom he was writing were living during the outbreak of the Archidamian War.

---

[23] Thus, for example, his protestations about the probity of Aristides in VIII. 79 (cf. 95) need to be seen in the proper perspective. They indicate not that Aristides was his '*Bürgerideal*' but probably that Aristides was unjustly maligned by Herodotus' contemporaries because of his connection with the assessment of the tribute for the Athenian league.

V

THE ARCHIDAMIAN WAR

BEFORE Felix Jacoby published his masterful essay on Herodotus and lent authority to the view of Herodotus which had been expounded by Eduard Meyer,[1] another and divergent conception of Herodotus' intent, there rejected, had been promoted by H. Nissen.[2] This interpretation held that Herodotus was not apologist for Athens but propagandist for peace, Herodotus attempted, according to this view, to make Sparta and Athens understand the folly of the Archidamian War by reminding these powers of the prior harmony and greatness fostered by their mutual co-operation. Such an interpretation of Herodotus' intent was easy to refute in this form. No contemporary who read his work would plausibly be moved by it to declare for peace. A more likely effect would be to make the reader regretfully submit to the necessity of a major clash between two states which even in 480–79 B.C. had not been in harmony. Herodotus does not idealize the mutual relations of these states; if he wished to point to the good old days he would have made them better.

Yet the very ease of Jacoby's refutation, which did strong duty in helping him to prop up the 'other' theory,[3] indicates how easily an important issue can be submerged by an apparently unexceptionable syllogistic approach. Jacoby rejected the conclusion that Herodotus wanted to promote an

---

[1] With modifications: see above, Chapter III, p. 42. Jacoby's discussion: *RE* Suppl. II. 356. 31ff.

[2] *Historische Zeitschrift* 63 (1889), 419f.

[3] Had Jacoby proceeded to consider that one factor militating against the 'panegyric' conception is that Athens herself is painted realistically (see, e.g., IX. 7), he would have seen that his own theory too was flawed.

end of war or to preclude the beginning of strife because of the demonstrable invalidity of the premise—that Herodotus idealized the former co-operation of Sparta and Athens. But what Jacoby should have recognized is that the conclusion about Herodotus' pacifistic intent actually is an inference from Herodotus' fundamental hatred of war.[4] And although the possible inference that Herodotus wished to promote peace is assailable because his work does not communicate the spirit of that intention or display a panegyric tendency, we are still left with Herodotus' hatred of war pre-eminently inspiriting his work, and it is not to be relegated into oblivion together with Nissen's theory. For if Herodotus' attitude to war is taken in conjunction with the manner of his description of the Greeks in 480–79 B.C., another possibility left unexplored by Jacoby naturally suggests itself. Hatred of war is compatible not only with the positive idea that peace should be promoted. It is also consistent with acceptance of war's necessity. When we recall that Herodotus' *Histories* are built on a determinative pattern, that he stressed Greek divisiveness in 480–79 B.C., and that he adumbrated a cyclical view of the rise and fall of the states of men,[5] the nature of his intentions are clearly pointed. He did not write to advocate peace. The sad recognition of necessity for war is the message inherent in his work.

It is an irony that the two chief interpretations of Herodotus' intent so thoroughly reject the clearest signs of it because of presuppositions with which it is incompatible. A distortive and arbitrary compartmentalization of Herodotus' 'aspects' is required because to take him as a whole would spell the end to either view. By making Herodotus a *Wahl-Athener*, he must approve of the Athenian Empire and justify the coming conflict. But this pits Herodotus' philosophy and view of history and love of freedom against himself. Similarly, his 'desire for peace' is incompatible with the conception of

---

[4] V. 97. 3 and VI. 98. 2 make explicit what is conveyed *passim.*

[5] See I. 5, 207. 2; cf. Schmid-Stählin, *Griechische Literaturgeschichte* I. 2. 618, n. 7.

human instability of which his work is the monument. It makes incomprehensible his description of the good old days as discordant. It will be noticed that both interpretations make Herodotus an optimistic soul at odds with the predominant truths of his entire work. And so Herodotus' 'message', which must be the mirror of his intent, has been detached from the *Histories* and filed away in a little box called 'his philosophy' because it does service to neither of these views and, more importantly, because it suggests another which is unpalatable to his modern audience.

Herodotus considered the events of his own time an unmitigated but thoroughly unavoidable disaster. It was the truth of this proposition which his *Histories* intended to convey. No other conclusion is possible when the historical vision of Herodotus, which he attempted to teach to his contemporaries, is taken into account.

The facts hardly require discussion, so familiar are they. In the beginning of Herodotus' history (I. 5. 4) comes the initial statement of what is programmatic for the entire work. Greatness is ephemeral; 'human happiness is never stable.' A supreme example is shortly thereafter provided in the Solon-Croesus episode.[6] From that point, as his history develops, one example after the next passes before our eyes until, with Xerxes' defeat, the *Histories* end on the note of the first retaliatory thrust of the Athenians at Sestus. The essential truth for Herodotus was ebb and flow. God will strike the highest tree without exception and, if necessary, without excuse. In most cases the *hybris* of man brings on his own downfall—as, for instance, with Cyrus or Cleomenes. In other cases, nothing but the malignancy or jealousy of God can explain it. States, like men, were caught in the same net. War was inevitable, if not for one reason then for another. With human nature as it is, acts of injustice were inescapable.

---

[6] The immense importance he attached to this episode as indicative of the meaning of his work best explains why the Lydian *logos* was placed in first position. See De Sanctis, *Studi di storia della storiografia greca, Il pensiero storico* 34 (Firenze, 1951), 53ff.

And to Herodotus it was apparent that once an unjust act is committed an endless sequence of action and counter-action will follow.

οὐδεὶς ἀνθρώπων ἀδικῶν τίσιν οὐκ ἀποτίσει.

So dreamed Hippias shortly before his expulsion from Athens (V. 56. 1), and foreign policy too was either based on vengeance or protection against it. Once started, the process could not be stopped. Thus Xerxes needed to avenge the defeat at Marathon and the destruction of the holy places at Sardes by destroying Athens (VII. 8 β). And Athens, with perfect consequence, would be obliged to repay Persia with a fitting vengeance. There was a constant struggle between men fighting to be free and others to enslave, with a constant shifting of role. Cyrus won freedom for the Persians and proceeded to impose slavery on others. It is no understatement to say that for Herodotus this was an immutable law of history.

All this is familiar enough. Yet two consequences follow from it which are important for our purposes. The first is simply that Herodotus was persuaded of the reality of his tragic view of history. It is not just an organizational scheme permitting him to bind up his history in tidy fashion. The later portions of his history, especially, were designed to show it, speeches were invented to clarify it, advisers were introduced to point it. Yet we tend to minimize the importance of his historical philosophy either by subjecting it to analysis intending to reveal its functional purpose as a 'unifying factor' or by 'explaining' his persuasion by reference to his literary antecedents. But the literary filiation, if interesting, is comparatively unimportant. It should not seduce us into forgetting that his conception of historical inevitability can only have grown out of his experience. Herodotus was not born with the view that we must read the final chapter before we judge of the happiness of man in preceding ones. If we choose to understand his philosophy as derivative of someone else like Solon, we must realize that such an identification provides no actual explanation of Herodotus' attachment to that view. He may have shared Solon's vision, but Solon's possession of it does not explain why Herodotus shared it. Although to us Herodotus' philosophy is little more than a literary chestnut, so familiar are we with it, to him it was an immutable truth of central importance for mankind.

A second consequence needs emphasis because we are so apt to detach Herodotus from the time in which he wrote and from the audience for which he wrote, assuming that like Thucydides he delivered himself to the general audience of the future. Just as his conception of human instability and the ideas connected with it were no literary motif to him, so also did his persuasion of its truth engender his desire to communicate it to his audience—not as a picturesque explanation of ancient history but as something of immediate importance to them. Herodotus' truths did not vanish away in 479 B.C.; 'there never was a man *nor ever will be* whose lot from birth is not mixed with evil, with the greatest evil reserved for the greatest men' (VII. 203. 2); Solon spoke not just for Croesus but for all the world (I. 86. 5). The desire of any man to instruct others about the meaning of the past carries with it the corollary that the knowledge gained is important to the present, and that is true particularly here where it is a matter of 'eternals'.[7] The conclusion cannot be avoided that Herodotus considered it important for his contemporaries to understand what he was trying to tell them because it was relevant to their time. When we consider the political situation then current, on the one hand, and the subject of VII–IX, on the other, that his account is about a war for freedom and centres on the Greek states currently embroiled, it is clear that it could only have been important for him to teach his contemporaries about themselves. His work

---

[7] The view that the Persian War was conceived by Herodotus as the 'final development of the ancient feud between Greek and barbarian', Pagel, *Die Bedeutung des aitiologischen Momentes* (Diss. Berlin 1927), p. 23, is unfounded.

was relevant to the great issues centring on the outbreak of war in 431 B.C.

Herodotus' intention was to make his listeners understand the crisis of the day in historical perspective. For this, like all the others, was a struggle against enslavement by an empire. Our sympathy for Athens will not, I hope, blind us to the truth of this contention. The proponents of the Empire will have had their special reasons for desiring Athenian control—the prospect of power, the overthrow of the 'few'—and these will no doubt have explained away the *douleia*, mitigated the *arche*, or at least have counted up the benefits such a rule could confer on them and their factions. But the question is not whether the Empire was an unmitigated evil for everyone. The point for our purposes is that the existence of the Athenian Empire and the threat of enslavement—limitation of autonomy like that effected by Cyrus for the Ionian Greeks, like that Xerxes would have effected for Athens by installing his partisans—were, so formulated, the crucial issues of the day. Herodotus' audience, moreover, was unsympathetic to Athens (VII. 139). And Herodotus is as devoted as anyone in the history of letters to the ideal of freedom. Freedom and empire were incompatible then as today. What is remarkable, consequently, about Herodotus' attitude to Athens is the sympathy he extended to her, which involved the recognition that her present situation was a consequence of her earlier greatness—not that her present position was intrinsically defensible because of that earlier achievement. And with this compassionate understanding he deplored that hatred of Athens which ignored completely the inherent tragedy of her position. To this extent one may agree with Jacoby that Herodotus wanted to remind people of Athens' earlier services to the cause of liberty. But he did not do it as a partisan of Athens or in order to justify or exonerate that state. He did it because in his opinion Athens had been caught in a sad and inevitable process bringing disaster to all of Greece, and it needed to be understood. Perhaps only an Ionian in culture who was a Dorian by blood could have been

so judicious. It does him a disservice to make him a propagandist of any kind when his intention was rather to communicate his own tragic view to a partisan audience roused
to animosity.

Herodotus' method of accomplishing his purpose is the
same as that observed in his treatment of Pausanias and
Themistocles. The knowledge and expectations of his audience are an essential presupposition for his narrative. Like
Pausanias and Themistocles,[8] Athens is left at the height of
her greatness prosecuting the war in 479 B.C. Surely that
sudden termination which has puzzled so many becomes in
this context comprehensible and eloquent even apart from
that parable in the final paragraph of his *Histories*. Let us
think ourselves back to the Archidamian War and ask what
our train of thought would be after reading that last portion
about Athens at Sestus, even if we missed the hint Herodotus
supplies (IX. 117 *ad fin.*)[9] In one quick and comprehensive
mental stride we would cover the intervening period—think
of Athens' league, the retaliatory war against Persia, the
reduction of rebellious subjects and transition to empire,
and, finally, the outbreak of another war begun for the sake
of freedom. And so we come full circle, sharing with Herodotus some of his sadness and pessimism.

Herodotus' audience could hardly have avoided making
some such connection of idea. Unlike us, they had no presuppositions about his historical method, automatically
accepted his dramatic technique, and could not have

[8] See VIII. 124. 1, where we take leave of Themistocles at the very summit of
his career.

[9] 'When autumn came and they were still besieging the place, the Athenians
became impatient since they were away from home and could not take the
fortification. They asked their generals to lead them back. But the generals said
that they would not until they took the place or until the Athenian government
summoned them. οὕτω δὴ ἐστεργον τὰ παρεόντα.' The position of οὕτω requires
that either we translate 'so greatly did the *soldiers* like the present situation,'
which is nonsense, or 'so greatly did the *generals* (or even τὸ κοινόν) like the
present situation.' The alternative meaning of στέργειν, 'to put up with',
makes no good sense with οὕτω. This allusion, like the reference to τὸ κοινόν,
has clear point: the Athenians are on the move. Herodotus has put it in a
nutshell.

compartmentalized the Athens and Sparta of the Persian War from the same states in their own time.[10] Herodotus, in any case, was not reluctant to point the ironies in such a way as to compel such juxtaposition, as one instructive episode, in VII. 157ff., indicates.

Here Herodotus took a remarkable liberty in the course of relating the story of the Greeks' attempt to enlist the support of Gelon in the imminent conflict. They urge reasons why Gelon should come to their assistance. Gelon, after some preliminary hesitation, decides to involve himself in the coming war and to do so on a staggering scale. 'I will supply two hundred triremes and twenty thousand hoplites and two thousand knights and two thousand archers and two thousand slingers and two thousand light horsemen. And I promise to provide food for the entire Greek army for as long as we shall fight. But I will do this on one condition: that I be the commander-in-chief of the Greeks in the war against the barbarian.' But Sparta would not hear of it and so Gelon compromised by settling for command over the navy. 'Gelon made that advance and before anyone else could say a word[11] the Athenian messenger answered him with these words: "O King of Syracuse, Greece has sent us to you not because we need a leader but because we need an army."' We Athenians, he continues, will not give up our hegemony to Syracusans. Gelon's reply is very fine. 'Friend Athenian,' he says, 'it seems that you will have rulers but no one to rule. Since then you insist on having the whole without compromise, the faster you go back to Greece the better.

---

[10] It is we who make the dichotomy between the one war, a victory, and the other, to us a defeat. Because of Thucydides' authority, it is a truism to us that the causes of the Peloponnesian War begin just after the end of the Persian. Yet this should not suggest that Herodotus and his contemporaries neatly separated the two—as Thucydides' own speeches attest (e.g., I. 73. 2). That Herodotus saw the entire period as a continuum is shown by VI. 98. That the entire period down to the death of Artaxerxes were three continuous generations of human misery indicates the connection he made between contemporary events and that prior triumph. Indeed, how otherwise could he have taken so grim a view of that 'splendid victory'?

[11] φθάσας δέ. The embellishment is important.

But tell them that you have taken the Spring out of the year.'

Herodotus' intent could not be clearer on several counts. The issue of hegemony was more important than national survival. This is the obvious point of the story; Herodotus' contemporaries would have understood it only too well. But even more striking is the fact that the words Gelon used— 'you have taken the Spring from the year'—were from the mouth of Pericles. More important yet, they were spoken in a funeral oration, probably that first oration delivered in the Peloponnesian War.[12] The appearance of this phrase in Herodotus guarantees that it was widely known, and no occasion would have attracted more interest than that first funeral oration following from the awesome beginning of the Peloponnesian War. The tenor of Pericles' speech and, especially, something so notable as that eloquent and pathetic phrase, would have circulated throughout the Hellenic world.

What, then, are we to conclude from Herodotus' adoption of Pericles' words and his conferring of them on Gelon? The consensus is that it is a compliment to Pericles. Only the assumption that Herodotus was an admirer of Pericles and, more particularly, that to quote him is automatically to compliment him can explain such an opinion. But the context of the remark demands a contrary inference. Gelon has said that since the Greeks, in their ambition for hegemony, insist on having the whole without compromise, their ambassadors are to go back to Greece and tell the people that they have taken the Spring out of the year. The remark makes little sense in the Herodotean context on the face of it, for the Athenian rejection of Gelon's offer achieves no such effect. But is it not apparent that it makes very grim sense

---

[12] The idea that the phrase derives from an oration delivered some ten years earlier rests on the belief, apparently, that Thucydides would have repeated the phrase if it had been uttered in the famous funeral oration. Aristotle's reference to the phrase certainly suggests that he is thinking of the well-known one (*Rhetoric* I. 7. 34), and the inference is confirmed by *Rhetoric* III. 10. 7, where Aristotle adds the qualifying words 'in the war'. That can only be the Archidamian War, not the conquest of Samos.

indeed when viewed from the perspective of the Archidamian War? No listener at that time could have missed the implication, and it is not nice. Gelon's reference to the Greek unwillingness to compromise, their insistence on 'having the whole', is directly linked to a phrase celebrating the first to die from the fraternal conflict centring on precisely that issue. The technique is incomparable; the effect is chilling.

The lamentable state of our historical record makes it impossible to trace other such allusions, if they exist, as very possibly they do.[13] But other allusions of patent irony abound though they are less concrete. In VIII. 140ff., for example, Herodotus describes an attempt made by Mardonius, through his agent Alexander of Macedon, to detach Athens from the Hellenic league. The Spartans fear treachery and send an embassy to Athens in order to dissuade the Athenians from taking any such step.[14] There was not the need: in that critical hour the Athenians deliver a spirited reply to Alexander. 'We very well know that the power of the Mede is far greater than our own. But even so we long for liberty and will fight as best we can. You should not attempt to persuade us to come to terms with the barbarian, nor will we do it. So now tell Mardonius this from the Athenians: So long as the sun keeps its present course we shall never come to terms with Xerxes. We will defend ourselves against him by attacking him, trusting in our allied gods and heroes whose shrines and statues he burned in disrespect.' To the Spartans, similarly, the Athenians made a forceful response in answer to the implication that they were even capable of treachery (VIII. 144). 'There is neither enough gold on earth nor land so beautiful and fertile that we would accept it in return for medizing and enslaving Greece. Many and great are the considerations that would stop us from doing so

---

[13] Some of the remarks in the speeches of Xerxes and Mardonius in VII. 8ff. look as if they could have been typical of Athenian rhetoric in the years before the war, especially 11. 2–4.

[14] See VIII. 142 for the Spartan speech. If ἀρχῆς (142. 2) is what Herodotus wrote, Herodotus has dropped the mask and is speaking directly to the issue. If not, the connection is still intimate enough.

even if we wished—most important, the burned and deva-
stated shrines and statues of the gods whom we must avenge
at all costs rather than come to terms with their destroyer,
and, secondly, the fact of common brotherhood, since we are
of the same blood and speak with the same tongue, possess
common shrines of the gods, common sacrifices, and common ways. These it would not be right for Athenians to betray. Know, then, if you do not already know it, we will
never come to terms with Xerxes as long as one Athenian is
left alive.'

It is customary to consider these speeches an idealistic
expression of Athenian love for liberty, to refer to this 'noble
assertion of Hellenic nationality'.[15] Noble it indeed would
be, if it were delivered or recorded in 479 B.C. But the matter
is more complex than this; our perspective is not that of
Herodotus or of his audience. Macan, in his commentary,
saw that all was not right even on a superficial level. His
objection[16] was to the fact that Herodotus 'appears quite
unconscious of the satire he thus levels against Athens' in
view of the immediately subsequent passage (IX. 11) in
which the Athenians threaten in their anger at Sparta that
they will become the allies of the Great King. He resolved
that dilemma by assuming that Herodotus was unconscious
of the satire levelled against Athens; that the 'two narratives
are from independent sources, and *more suo* he gives them
both, without adjustment, for what they are worth.'

That is, certainly, one way out of the dilemma. Is it
reasonable? The separation between Books VIII and IX is
not Herodotus',[17] and the entire narrative is one continuous
whole. Herodotus certainly knew what he was doing; the
interpretation of this author's intent cannot be reduced to
a helpless gesture. We have no alternative but to assume that

[15] How, ad loc.

[16] At VIII. 144, line 16.

[17] The separation between the μέν clause concluding VIII and the δέ
clause beginning IX is as artificial as the division of this unified episode into two
halves.

what in Herodotus is the second phase of Mardonius' negoti-
ations was intended as a pendant to the first. Herodotus is indeed making the Athenians contradict themselves. Even if
he had not gone so far as to underscore the irony, it is clear
that the brave words of the Athenians are double-edged
enough when viewed from the perspective of Herodotus and
his contemporaries. Athens made peace with Persia to gain
land and gold. The burned shrines were rebuilt by Pericles
with imperial revenues. Those common bonds linking Greek
to Greek were snapped by the outbreak of war between them.
These speeches can only be taken at face value by utterly
divorcing Herodotus from his milieu and by assuming that
he had no conception at all of the predictable thoughts of his
contemporaries. That assumption is incompatible with the
essence of his technique.

Enough has been said, I hope, to indicate that Herodotus'
method conjoins with his intent to yield a masterpiece of
irony and tragedy dominated by the contemporary spectre of
the Peloponnesian War.[18] Now, if we regard the *Histories* in
this light, it becomes possible to attempt an answer to the
question which earlier was posed. What led Herodotus to
become the historian of the monograph on Xerxes' War and
the author of the entire work as cast in its final form?

The crucial factor can only have been the prospect or
the outbreak of the war of 431 B.C. Though the idea of completing his account of the expansion of the Persian Empire
by a discussion of Xerxes' repulse in 480–79 B.C. was
implicit in that subject, the final chapter of that history became a subject in its own right. The contemporary conflict, I
suggest, made him view the other with new significance, precisely the significance we have seen reflected in it. The final
episode of one subject had become intrinsically important
in its own right, the first chapter of another. The empire of

---

[18] Is IX. 27. 4 ironical? IX. 90, with the highly rhetorical sentence of
Hegesistratus of Samos ('calling on the gods they shared in common, he urged
them to defend these men, who were Greeks, from slavery, and to ward off the
barbarian'), invites the thought of the conquest of Samos by Athens in 440 B.C.

Xerxes was turned away but the empire of Athens was born. The necessity for the Greek world to unite first opened the question of hegemony and the long process of continuing the war chafed it into a wound. As Herodotus viewed it, it was the pre-history of the Peloponnesian War.

With that shift of view-point came also a corresponding shift in the themes preoccupying him, though the difference is subtle. The central theme, now, in VII–IX, is the quest for freedom by disunited states threatened by an imperial power. Earlier Herodotus was content to adduce the specific motives prompting Persia's imperialistic advance. Now the psychology behind the expansion of nations rather than the specific causes of Persian conquest is the major issue. Herodotus was a witness to history repeating itself and so, in his search for causes turned from the specific to the general and emphasized the eternally relevant motives as he judged them from his own time. The difference in approach can be seen by comparing the explanation given by Herodotus for the march against Croesus by Cyrus (I. 75), the causes of the Ionian Revolt (V. 30ff.) and the invasion of Attica commanded by Darius (VI. 94) with those presented for the reader in the beginning of VII. 8ff. In the earlier cases, Herodotus was content with a pragmatic explanation; in VII the speeches of Xerxes, Mardonius, and Artabanus— speeches which because of their position as well as weight are programmatic of the themes Herodotus wished to impress on his reader—these speeches make plain that what is being explored is the impulse on the part of the successful to extend their successes (Xerxes) and the inevitability of failure implicit in such a course (Artabanus). The specific cause of the final conflict, those injuries done the Persians by the Greeks, becomes secondary in interest to the consideration of the remorseless drive of an empire to extend itself with or without provocation. The new interest, for Herodotus, is the general question of imperialism.

What Herodotus has done in VII in the speeches of Xerxes and his advisers is to fuse the specific motive with the eternal ones relevant to his own time and to Athens' course. He is characterizing more than Xerxes and Persia's empire. Thus Xerxes indeed wants to destroy Athens to exact vengeance for the defeat at Marathon and the desecration of the shrines at Sardes (VII. 8 β). But he also wanted to conquer Greece because he believed 'that no other city of men or race of men will then remain which could come to battle with these removed as enemies. And thus the guilty will have their yoke of slavery—*and the innocent too*' (VII. 8 γ. 3). That last remark is surprising because it is so gratuitous. Xerxes is not presented as an amoral character, yet the remark is amoral. It suggests that Herodotus is thinking beyond the specific. Perhaps the remark can be explained by understanding it as a little indication of the *hybris* of Xerxes that helps to prepare for his fall. But Xerxes' speech is not pointed in that direction; that larger issues are involved is clearly revealed by the speech of Artabanus. The task is not to render intelligible to the Greeks the cause of Persian attack. It is to explain the cancerous nature of imperialism; to show how inevitably moral corruption is entailed by it.

Herodotus is thinking generically. He is interpreting the past by the present. In similar fashion his account of the Greek resistance to Persia gives point to contemporary animosities. The emphasis on the constant division between Sparta and Athens, indeed, between all the Greeks, can only be explained by the later animosity and his readiness to see the past in terms of it. Hence his attitude to Corcyra (VII. 168) and that curious incident centring on a heated and petty dispute between the Athenians and the Tegeans at the very moment prior to the deadly serious battle of Plataea (IX. 26ff.). Here the competing virtues of Peloponnesians and Ionians are voiced as they might have been during the Archidamian War.[19] We should not suppose that Herodotus

---

[19] The final remark of the Athenians in IX. 27. 6 is notable because it is so oddly docile. Herodotus does not conceive of the Athenians as a submissive people (see, e.g., VIII. 3; IX. 27 itself, 102). They nevertheless end by saying that 'it is not right for us to quarrel at this time because of the battle order. We are willing, Lacedaemonians, to do your will' (IX. 27. 6). Herodotus is not

was an automaton reproducing naïvely the animosities of his sources. Rather is he exploiting them. His account is the mirror of those animosities (see IX. 54. 1) as well as the harbinger of the final clash, and his references to them are keyed to it.[20]

Perhaps we can go further. The conception of historical inevitability revealed by Herodotus is easy to take for granted as if it were self-evident to him or as if he borrowed the idea from his 'predecessors'. Though the latter idea can be dismissed, the former deserves attention. For Herodotus was evidently the first to lock a series of wars into a causal framework reaching far into the past. *He* imposed the determinative pattern. Yet this concept of historical inevitability is not something than can be acquired by a study of the past. With enough history to study, it is possible to identify certain patterns. So with Herodotus, the Persian War was a particular instance of a recurring phenomenon. But the inevitability of that repetition is an idea neither inherent nor suggested by the facts themselves. Herodotus could have learned from a study of his material that Persia made a constant advance spanning the lives of several rulers. That advance could be seen as a continuous process, each conquest triggered by a particular cause. The idea, however, that this process was inevitable because of the nature of things—that Persia had to advance for reasons transcending specific causes—that could not be learned from the study of these facts. It can only have been projected back into the pattern as a 'truth' learned from the present. And if he learned it from the present, the vital factor must have been the coming of the Archidamian

---

more suo, contradicting his own conceptions. The Athenians are in leash, waiting for bigger game—οὐ γὰρ ἐν τῷ τοιῷδε τάξιος εἵνεκα στασιάζειν πρέπει are the crucial words. The time for them to change their approach comes in IX. 106.

[20] Thus, for example, his quotation of the Athenian slander of Adeimantus (VIII. 94), which concludes with the statement that the Athenian version of his cowardice is incompatible with the testimony of the rest of Greece is an illustration not of his blind and naïve devotion to Athenian dogma but an indication of his ease in shifting from the description of the actual clashes of that early time to allusions to contemporary hatreds.

War. Perhaps because of the broadening influence of travel
and study, perhaps because of his inherent nature, his Dorian
and Ionian ties—for some reason or many, Herodotus was
extraordinarily unprejudiced. With his sympathy for Athens
and for Sparta he could see neither side as the villain of his
day; in spite of Athens' empire he could not simply fix the
blame for the present crisis on that state. Both sides, he well
knew, were capable of pettiness and greatness; more than
pettiness or jealousy was responsible for this clash. How could
two states, linked by so much, have fallen into a course
which must end in the destruction of one of them, and why
could they not break away from it? His contemplation of
what must have appeared to him to be the inevitable approach of that crisis led him to the revelation that crises of
this kind are not self-induced but are built into the nature of
things, follow from an endless chain of prior causes, all because of human nature. Thus his history was born out of his
passionate involvement in the great crisis of his time.[21]

Herodotus' admiration for Athens as the cultural leader of
the Greeks, and as one of the two forces that in 480–79 B.C.
had worked the miracle of repelling Xerxes, cannot have
been unmixed with disapproval of her present course. The
ethics of the historian are incompatible with oppression. His
standpoint was that of a pan-Hellenist; he was a partisan of
no particular state. But because of his sympathy for Athens he
sought to comprehend the devolution, as he must have considered it, of this city. All that he had learned about history,
all that he had seen about the way man reacts, combined to
show him how triumph brings a momentum leading to
egoism and excess. The present tragedy was built on an
earlier triumph and literally required that triumph in order

----

[21] Herodotus said it all in VIII. 3: the Athenians recognized in 480 B.C. that
their hopes for hegemony were better suppressed in view of the opposition
raised to it by the other allies. Herodotus approved. If there was a quarrel about
this matter of hegemony, 'Greece would be brought to ruin . . . for internal
strife is a thing as much worse than war carried on by a united people, as war
itself is worse than peace' (Rawlinson's translation).

to evolve. So Herodotus became the historian of the Persian War with the recognition of the equivocal meaning this victory would imply for later times. He wrote his history in order to explain that inevitable and tragic ambiguity which is the essence of his work.

EPILOGUE

THE credibility of the argument presented in the preceding chapters must depend, in the final analysis, on comparatively simple considerations. Is it more likely, in the first place, that Herodotus wrote the work in the form in which we have it by responding to a variety of challenges confronting him during the period of his creativity or is it preferable to suppose that the *Histories* is a less adventitious creation corresponding to an initial purpose? Secondly, is the interpretation of Herodotus' intent and method as ironic and dramatic preferable to the traditional view which holds that he was at the mercy of his informants and incapable of maintaining self-consistency?

That Herodotus developed as he wrote and shifted his intentions as he developed is an assumption justified by indications present in his work. It is also intrinsically likely. He lived in an age when 'genres' were fluid, when experimentation was the norm. He learned as he lived and he may be supposed to have been influenced by what he learned. That the *Histories* betray the record of Herodotus' advance from apprenticeship to mastery and from intelligence to wisdom is irrelevant to the question of the 'unity' of the work. To the extent that the champions of aesthetical integrity have made Herodotus' achievement self-explanatory, that achievement has been obscured.

Herodotus' intent and method, as I have attempted to elucidate them, are sophisticated, though unconventional if they be judged in the light of what 'history' eventually became. Herodotus could not predict that development. He could not expect that his work would be viewed through a lens ground for the study of the 'scientific'

historians who would follow him. The usual view of Herodotus follows from an insistence that he be typical, and is informed by the notion that the mental attitudes he brought
with him to Egypt in his early days were substantially the
same in his prime.

The traditional conception of Herodotus makes him the
inconsequent author of a work which, even with the alleged
blemishes, is a great history. The qualities attributed to
Herodotus, abstractly considered, may seem plausible, if
somewhat overdrawn. He is naïve, credulous, unconscious
of incompatibilities, loyal to one state but at the mercy of
those who impugn it. Yet, as I have tried to show, if we are
less supererogatory and take him at his word, these charges
fall to the ground.

Herodotus is not as simple as he is made to appear. He
was capable of irony and aimed at dramatic effect. Above all,
he knew full well the *Tendenz* he is supposed merely to reflect.
A Greek who has travelled through the world, visited the
major cities of Hellas, lived in Athens and Sparta, watched the
war approach, talked to the leading figures, investigated
the earlier history of the Hellenic world, mingled in Thouria
with opponents and proponents of Athens and Sparta, listened
to Corinthians, Aeginetans, Thebans, Samians, cannot be
the construct we have made him. Herodotus is responsible
for the objectionable contradictions; it is we who make
Herodotus simple.

The difference attitude can make is startling. Herodotus'
contemporaries heard Herodotus and read him without any
of the barriers which the later Greeks and the moderns have
so painstakingly erected when the Persian War could be
idealized and Herodotus became a 'classic'. They judged
him from his work without attempting to explain the work in
terms of its position in the family tree of historiography. We
too should regard him without such prejudice.

INDEX OF NAMES AND SUBJECTS

INDEX OF MORE IMPORTANT PASSAGES